Loving the Questions

An Exploration of the Nicene Creed

Marianne H. Micks

COWLEY PUBLICATIONS
Cambridge ✦ Boston
Massachusetts

Trinity Press International
Valley Forge, Pennsylvania

Published in the United States of America jointly by Trinity Press International and Cowley Publications, a division of the Society of St. John the Evangelist. No portion of this book may be reproduced, stored in or introduced into a retrieval system, or transmitted, in any form or by any means—including photocopying—without the prior written permission, except in the case of brief quotations embodied in critical articles and reviews.

International Standard Book Number: 1-56101-081-2
Library of Congress Number: 93-22816

Library of Congress Cataloging-in-Publication Data
Micks, Marianne H.
   Loving the questions: an exploration of the Nicene Creed/
     Marianne H. Micks.
      p. cm.
   Includes bibliographical references.
   ISBN 1-56101-081-2
   1. Nicene Creed.   I. Title.
   BT999.M53 1993
   238'.142—dc20   93-22816

This book is printed on acid-free recycled paper and was produced in the United States of America.

Cover illustration is taken from a fifth-century mosaic vault decoration in the mausoleum of Galla Pacidia, Ravenna.

Trinity Press International
P. O. Box 851
Valley Forge, Pennsylvania 19482

Cowley Publications
28 Temple Place
Boston, Massachusetts 02111

For Rosemari
and all my former students

Contents

The Nicene Creed

We believe in one God,
  the Father, the Almighty,
  maker of heaven and earth,
    of all that is, seen and unseen.

We believe in one Lord, Jesus Christ,
  the only Son of God,
  eternally begotten of the Father,
  God from God, Light from Light,
  true God from true God,
  begotten, not made,
  of one Being with the Father.
  Through him all things were made.
  For us and for our salvation
    he came down from heaven:
  by the power of the Holy Spirit
    he became incarnate from the Virgin Mary,
    and was made man.
  For our sake he was crucified under Pontius Pilate;
    he suffered death and was buried.
  On the third day he rose again
    in accordance with the Scriptures;
  he ascended into heaven
    and is seated at the right hand of the Father.
  He will come again in glory
    to judge the living and the dead,
    and his kingdom will have no end.

We believe in the Holy Spirit, the Lord,
the giver of life,
who proceeds from the Father and the Son.
With the Father and the Son
he is worshiped and glorified.
He has spoken through the Prophets.

We believe in one holy catholic
and apostolic Church.
We acknowledge one baptism
for the forgiveness of sins.
We look for the resurrection of the dead,
and the life of the world to come. Amen.

Chapter 1

Asking the Questions

We believe....

E very Sunday thousands of Christians rise to their feet in churches around the world to say or sing that simple phrase. In the original Greek it is one word (*pisteuōmen*), as it was also for centuries in the West when Latin was the language of the liturgy. What kind of declaration is this? What did the three paragraphs this phrase introduces mean when they were written, and what do they mean today?

The Nicene Creed is a statement of Christian faith adopted by what is called the first great ecumenical council in 325 and expanded at a later conference in Constantinople in 381. Gradually it found its way into the eucharistic liturgy, first in the East and later in the West. By 1014 the creed was a regular part of the Roman Mass on Sundays and festivals. Now it is recited by the congregation directly after the sermon, which follows the reading of the gospel for the day.

The words "we believe" that introduce the Nicene Creed are of immense importance. *We* are making a statement about the nature of the faith of the Christian church; it is more of a community statement than a personal statement. We are describing in summary form the One in whom Christians put their trust. In the process we are using a language hallowed by some seventeen hundred years of use—hallowed and also handicapped by that history.

Because it was framed in another age, using the categories of thought that are no longer ours, the Nicene Creed seems out of date to many of us now. It raises a number of questions for today's believer. Unlike the Apostles' Creed, which was written in the first-person singular and used at baptisms, the Nicene Creed was originally intended to rule out certain heretical ways of thinking, especially about the person of Jesus Christ. Although it is seldom used today as a test for orthodoxy, the Nicene Creed is still accepted as a normative statement of what the Christian church believes. In the Chicago-Lambeth Quadrilateral, which sets forth the fundamental bases for Christian unity, the Nicene Creed is called "the sufficient statement of Christian faith."

Many modern Christians have, I think, one of three chief reactions to reciting the creed. Some resign themselves to meaningless, indeed "vain" repetition. We don't know what it means, but it is given in the inherited form of worship, so we will assume it serves some ritualistic purpose, perhaps that of a powerful mantra or incantation. Alternatively, others privately decide to recite just as much of it as they can without sacrificing intellectual integrity: sure, I believe in one God, but I don't like the sexist metaphor Father. Or, I am willing to say I believe Jesus was born of the Virgin Mary, if you mean by that only that she was a young girl, not biologically a virgin. All of us would want to make private provisos of this sort from time to time if we were in fact stating our individual belief.

The third reaction is equally widespread, and it involves looking for a denomination that doesn't use ancient creeds in worship. Many of these churches have produced statements of faith in modern English that are appealing to modern sensibilities. One such recent *credo*, for example, adds a healthy concern for social justice to its expression of common faith and emphasizes the ministry of the man Jesus and the quality of his life, which is totally ignored by the inherited text. Of Jesus it says, "We trust in Jesus Christ, God with us in human flesh, who proclaimed the reign of God: he preached good news to the poor and release to the captives; he healed the sick and ate with outcasts; he forgave sinners and called all people to repent and believe." When speaking of trust in God the Holy Spirit, it says, "In a broken and fearful world the Spirit gives us power to witness to Christ as Lord and Savior, to work for justice, freedom and peace, to smash the idols of church and culture, and to claim all life for Christ."[1] This new emphasis makes great sense.

All three of these personal reactions, however, ignore the fact that the Nicene Creed is a statement rooted in history, binding generation to generation at all times and in all places. Better, it is a synopsis of the Christian story, a recitation of the mighty acts of God as Christians understand them. Granted that it was forged in controversy, the creed's primary purpose today is not to root out the heretics from our midst. It is to celebrate the fact that God has raised up for us a mighty salvation. We have cause to rejoice.

Are we meant to shelve all our doubts and uncertainties as we recite the ancient words, then? By no means. Worshiping God does not mean turning off our minds. Quite the contrary. Within the context of faith all sorts of questions arise, and they should. A faith unventilated by doubt is as stuffy as a closed room. Doubt, as Geddes MacGregor argued in his book *Christian Doubt*, is an implicate of faith. As someone else once wisely said, "I respect faith, but doubt is what gets you an education."

The late Bernard Lonergan, a well-known Roman Catholic theologian, implied much the same thing when he wrote, "When an animal has nothing to do, it goes to sleep. When [a human being] has nothing to do, [he or she] may ask questions....The first moment is an awakening to one's intelligence. It is release from the dominance of biological drive and from the routine of everyday living. It is the effective emergence of wonder, of the desire to understand."[2]

Theologians as different as Augustine of Hippo, Anselm of Canterbury, and Charles Schulz of "Peanuts" fame have long celebrated the necessity of asking questions in the search for truth. In contrast to Tertullian, another North African theologian, who said that he believed Christianity because it was absurd (that is, simply did not accord with everyday common sense), Augustine as well as Anselm embraced the idea of faith seeking understanding. Augustine said he believed in order to understand. He started his justly famous *Confessions* with a whole string of questions to and about God. In the very second paragraph, for example, Augustine addresses six questions directly to God:

> But how can I call unto my God, my God and Lord? For in calling unto Him, I am calling Him to me: and what room is there in me for my God, the God who made heaven and earth? Is there anything in me, O God, that can contain You?...And if You are already in me, since otherwise I should not be, why do I cry to You to enter into me?...Where do I call You to come to, since I am in You? Or where else are You that You can come to me?[3]

Charles Schulz once pictured Peppermint Patti making a report to her class in school. In four successive frames of the comic strip Patti says, "My topic today is the purpose of theology. When discussing theology we must always keep our purpose in mind. Our purpose as students is understandably selfish. There is nothing better than being in a class where no one knows the answer."

Patti is right. Parroting the correct answer is not what being a thinking Christian is about. It is about asking questions, polishing the questions, honing them until they are a sharp expression of what you wonder about. It is about loving the questions. That is the advice the poet Rainer Maria Rilke once gave a young poet. "I want to beg you, as much as I can, dear sir, to be patient towards all that is unsolved in your heart, and try to love *the questions themselves*."[4]

Have you ever noticed how many questions Jesus asks in the gospels? Questioning appears to be a favorite mode of teaching for him, a way to start people thinking. The hymnodist William Chatterton Dix is one hundred percent wrong in the second verse of his familiar "Alleluia, sing to Jesus," which says, "Alleluia, he is near us, faith believes, nor questions how."

To imagine how important theological controversy was in the fourth century, at the time the Nicene Creed was being written, we need to watch television coverage of a pro-choice or pro-life rally, perhaps, or a protest over the issue of police brutality. As far as we know, the creed did not lead to rioting in the street, but feelings were equally intense over questions like "Was the incarnate Word of God fully God or some lesser being?" Men made up songs on the subject of the Incarnation and sang them to bawdy tunes in the barber shops. Women chatted about theology in their boudoirs, according to one ancient male theologian. The general unrest caused the emperor Constantine to call a conference of bishops in 325. He had a political crisis on his hands; the peace of the empire was threatened by dissension in the church.

The conference was held at the site of the emperor's summer palace, the Camp David of its day. The invitation to the conference has survived. He decided on Nicea, Constantine said, "both because the bishops from Italy and the rest of the countries of Europe are coming, and because of the excellent temperature of the

6

air, and in order that I may be present as a spectator and participator in those things which will be done."[5] The Bishop of Rome was not himself present, but he sent two representatives, and it is believed that two bishops came from as far away as Britain.

An eyewitness account of the proceedings has also come down to us from Eusebius, Bishop of Caesarea in Palestine. It is in the form of a letter written to his diocese, defending his own actions at the synod, and contains our earliest extant text of the Nicene Creed. It is a statement of faith designed to rule out the position of Arius, a North African priest and theologian who claimed that the Word of God was not fully God, co-eternal with the Father. Arius was worried that the unity of God was somehow in danger if God's Word, or Logos, was with God from the beginning, as John's gospel claims. His opponents thought that only someone fully God had the power to save humanity. Eusebius tried to convince his flock that the creed already in use in their own diocese was the basis of the new ecumenical statement of faith, although modern historians question this claim.

In any case, Eusebius makes it clear that he was not enthusiastic about the use of the crucial term about the Word of God, *homoousios*, which we now translate "One in Being" with the Father. What this means we will look at again when we discuss the question, "Who is the Christ?" For the present, we should note that according to Eusebius, the emperor himself took an active part in the discussion of theological fine points (he was probably under the guidance of his theological adviser, Hosius, a Spanish bishop), and that the emperor did endorse the inclusion of the decisive term, even though it was a word not found in the Bible. Most of the bishops did not think that a Christian needed to believe anything not said in the Holy Scriptures.

Dorothy L. Sayers has written a delightful play about the council called *The Emperor Constantine*. She presents a very convincing reconstruction of the ecclesiastical politics that fueled the conflict, which really began in Alexandria in Egypt with a quarrel between Bishop Alexander of that city and Arius, who was one of his presbyters. Sayers's portrayal of the council leaves one wondering if the bishop might have been jealous of Arius's popularity as a preacher. Other interpreters see the conflict rooted in different theological teaching in the University of Antioch and the University of Alexandria, similar to the different theological emphases of universities and seminaries today.

Whatever the causes of the Arian controversy, it was by no means ended by the Council of Nicea. A schism developed in the church immediately after the council ended, and Arian Christians feuded with Catholic Christians until the end of the fifth century. At one time much of Europe was in Arian hands.

We should note that the Creed of Nicea originally ended abruptly with the words, "and in the Holy Spirit." The third paragraph of the creed was expanded by the Council of Constantinople in 381 in order to say more about the Holy Spirit. Properly speaking, therefore, the creed should be called the Nicene-Constantinopolitan Creed, although it is virtually impossible to wrap one's tongue around that title.

Appended to the original document is a long list of opinions about the Son of God which, in the language of the time, "the catholic and apostolic Church anathematizes." Included were the opinions about Christ, the Word of God, attributed to Arius—statements such as "There was when he was not" or that he is "of another substance or essence" than God, or that he was created, changeable, and alterable. Clearly this creed was not written as a hymn of praise to the Triune God, but as a way to define orthodox faith and to exclude heretics. Over the centuries, however, the recitation of the creed became a regular part of the eucharistic liturgy.

Gradually, therefore, the creed came to serve a doxological as well as a "recapitulatory" function in worship.[6] It was primarily a way of praising God and of reinforcing the faith. In one rite it is introduced with the bidding, "Let us say with our lips the faith we believe in our heart." A contemporary writer expresses the same idea when he likens recitation of the creed to repounding the nails that work loose in the clapboards of his New Hampshire home. (My own Vermont house knows the same phenomenon in response to extremes of temperature.) "One of the great joys of repeating the Christian creed is that it gives us an opportunity to reaffirm the central truths of God's revelation," Gordon MacDonald writes. "As we say, 'I believe'...we begin to hammer back the nails of our convictions and commitments."[7]

Unfortunately the creed that was intended by the first great ecumenical council to bring peace to the church has succeeded in having some very divisive effects. Quite apart from the prolonged Arian controversy that created a centuries-long schism in the church, the language of the creed led to a further rift caused by the unilateral action of the western church in adding one word, *filioque*, to the third paragraph. This Latin word, asserting that God the Spirit proceeds from the Father **and the Son**, was probably added by the Council of Toledo in 589. The reason for the addition is obscure. It came gradually to be included more widely in churches of the West, as liturgical manuscripts were copied, but it was never accepted in the Eastern Orthodox churches. During Charlemagne's reign the *filioque* became a source of intense controversy between the Franks and the Byzantines, and it has remained a stumbling-block to Christian unity ever since. Many present-day ecumenists think it should be removed from the creed on historical grounds, if for no other reason, and we will explore the theological issues in a later chapter.

Finally, something must be said in this introductory chapter about the language of the creed. The current translation was agreed upon by the International Consultation on English Texts, an international and ecumenical group. Such common texts mean that throughout the English-speaking world Christians who use the Nicene Creed will be saying the same words in their worship, an important contribution toward ecumenical understanding. Apart from this kind of unity in the language, however, we need to be aware of the considerable diversity in the kinds of language used in these three short paragraphs. We have the language of fact and the language of metaphor. To say that Jesus was crucified under Pontius Pilate, suffered death, and was buried is clearly a historical fact. There is no ambiguity here. We are affirming an event that can be dated fairly precisely from extra-biblical sources. One word, *homoousios* or "One in Being," to which we have already referred, is a technical philosophical term in Greek ontology and still intelligible as such to metaphysical thinkers. Most of the rest of the creed is metaphorical.

All theological language is borrowed language, of course. We use words borrowed from everyday human experience to talk about God. We can say what God is not, and we have a whole string of inherited words that attempt just that. Theologians have a technical vocabulary, just as meteorologists or engineers or chemists or specialists do in any branch of human knowledge. As Thomas Aquinas, another great question-raiser of the past, put it, "For what He is not is clearer than what He is. Therefore similitudes drawn from things farthest away from God form within us a truer estimate that God is above whatsoever we may say or think of Him."[8]

God is not finite, for example, nor limited in power, nor confined by time and space, as we are. But even in these cases we are drawing on our own experience of the opposite situation. When we try to say what God is, the analogical character of our language is even more obvious. God is love, for example; God's love is like our love but infinitely more so. The metaphor "Father" may be the most blatant example, and one currently raising

11

the most vocal objections in the churches; to attribute any personal pronoun to God raises gender questions of the most troublesome sort. Clearly we need an English word that means she or he, one without a slash mark.

The creed also asserts, of course, that Christ will come again and that Christ's kingdom will have no end. Feminists are increasingly critical of using the word "kingdom" or any other monarchial language about God. One of the most articulate of these is Sallie McFague, author of *Models of God: Theology for an Ecological Nuclear Age*. No matter what joy surges through us when we sing the "Hallelujah" chorus from Handel's *Messiah*, the image of King of Kings and Lord of Lords is both powerful and dangerous, McFague argues with fine passion. No matter how ancient a metaphorical tradition may be and how firmly rooted in Scripture and tradition, it "must be discarded if it threatens the continuation of life itself."[9] In her judgment, monarchial metaphors for God lead us also to "lord it over" the planet earth.

Much of the language of the Nicene Creed is the monarchial language that McFague deplores, and it reflects the idea of a three-story universe of heaven, earth, and hell that demythologizers have long wanted us to update. No modern person, at least no one other than a literalist, thinks that heaven is "up"—so that in the Incarnation God "came down from heaven"—any more than they believe that God the Father has a left hand and a right hand. It is quite probable that no bishop at Nicea did either. Just because we live in the space age, we need not assume that our forebears were all incapable of recognizing metaphors when they used them.

Picture language has power. That is why poetry can say things that speak at once to human hearts and human heads. There is much to be said for the suggestion that we should read and recite the creed as if it were poetry, or at least poetic narrative. It is far closer to the great poetic voice of the prophet Isaiah, for example, than it is to the *Summa* of Thomas Aquinas: "In the year that King Uzziah died, I saw the Lord, high and lifted up, and his train filled the temple..." (Is. 6:1).

In this chapter I have stressed the importance of all Christians ventilating their faith with continuing doubts, expressed in an ongoing series of questions. I have also suggested that the Nicene Creed recited every Sunday in worship can provide a thought-provoking focus of such questions, but that it need not itself express one's individual belief. On the contrary, it is a statement of the faith of the whole church, rooted in the history of the fourth century. One avenue toward understanding that statement is to learn more about the intellectual crisis that called forth the council at Nicea that produced this creed. In subsequent chapters we will raise detailed questions about each of the three paragraphs of the ancient text that is now a regular part of our liturgy.

Endnotes

1. "A Proposed Brief Statement of Reformed Faith," *Theology Today* 45 (July 1988), p. 152.

2. Bernard Lonergan, *Insight: A Study of Human Understanding* (San Francisco: Harper & Row, 1977), p. 10.

3. Augustine of Hippo, *Confessions* 1. 1.

4. Rainer Maria Rilke, *Letters to a Young Poet* (New York: W. W. Norton, 1934), pp. 33-34.

5. J. Stevenson & W. H. C. Frend, *A New Eusebius: Documents Illustrating the History of the Church to AD 337*, rev. ed. (London: SPCK, 1989), p. 338.

6. Geoffrey Wainwright, *Doxology: The Praise of God in Worship, Doctrine, and Life* (Oxford: Oxford University Press, 1980), p. 186.

7. Gordon MacDonald, *Ordering Your Private World* (Nashville: Thomas Nelson, 1984), p. 168.

8. Thomas Aquinas, *Summa Theologica*, Question I, Article 9.

9. Sallie McFague, *Models of God: Theology for an Ecological Nuclear Age* (Philadelphia: Fortress Press, 1987), pp. 63ff.

Chapter 2

Who is God?

*We believe in God,
the Father, the Almighty....*

I n the checkout line at the grocery a few years ago, I saw the question "Who is God?" emblazoned across the cover of *Life*. Although not a regular reader of the magazine, I bought a copy. Inside were fascinating replies to that question given by people around the world. The people interviewed ranged from a convicted murderer now in prison to Archbishop Desmond Tutu, from a Florida farmer to a Hindu beggar with leprosy, from a second-grader in Iowa to a sixty-seven-year-old woman dying of cancer.

The variety of their answers matched the diversity of their lives. Yet the dominant picture of the Supreme Being reflected in these answers to our question is of a compassionate God, a God who cares. That conviction is evident from statements of people poles apart, from the murderer's "What impresses me now is the mercy of God" to the second-grader's "God makes people's lives better. He made my dad be a pushover. He buys me more toys than my mom."

The initial answer of the Nicene Creed to the question, "Who is God?" is given in the first two phrases: we believe in *one God, the Father, the Almighty*. Nowhere are the Jewish roots of Christianity more evident than in this radical insistence on monotheism. The words are an echo of the *Shema*, the text of Deuteronomy 6:4, "Hear, O Israel: the Lord is our God, the Lord alone." These words became the prayer that every devout Jew recited morning and night. Jews also wrote them on the doorposts of their houses, as Deuteronomy commands. The gospels make it clear that this fundamental of Judaism was also very much part of Jesus' faith. When one of the scribes asked him, for instance, "Which commandment is first of all?" Jesus answered, "The first is 'Hear, O Israel: the Lord our God, the Lord is one...'" (Mk. 12:29).

After insisting on monotheism in a culture in which polytheism was everywhere, the creed goes on to attribute two titles to this one being—Father and *Pantocrator*, the Almighty. It is exciting to focus on the punctuation reintroduced in the latest English translation of the original Greek, adopted by the international, ecumenical committee on English texts. It offers an enormous improvement for our understanding of who God is. We no longer say (as we used to) that we believe in *the Father Almighty*; we say instead *the Father, the Almighty*. This change liberates us from our stereotypical picture of God as a white-bearded omnipotent patriarch wielding a royal scepter, and it also affirms something markedly different about the divine nature.

A far richer understanding of the nature of divine being is conveyed by those seemingly minor translation
changes. They help us encounter and express dimensions of Holy Being not conveyed by the older English
texts. Not only do they better capture the sense of the
original Greek, they also tell us much about the Holy
God who is revealed in the Bible. Both the comma and
the definite article deserve attention.

The word translated "the Almighty" is *Pantocrator* in
the original Greek, a word difficult to translate accurately. It is a title in its own right, not just an adjective
describing the nature of God's fatherhood. By the addition of the article preceded by the comma, furthermore,
we are asserting two complementary things about the
nature of the Godhead rather than one. And the com-
plementarity of the two terms conveys, on closer in-
spection, a basic understanding of holiness—one in
complete accord with Rudolf Otto's classic study of the
phenomenon of holiness. God the Father, the Almighty
is both friendly and strange, both immensely attractive
and immensely awesome.

If we bring those two dimensions of the being of
God together by saying "God the Father Almighty" or
absorb one into the other too readily, it impoverishes
our understanding of who God is. That comma and
that definite article are good theology. Both the meaning of the two nouns and the link between the two deserve further attention.

The idea of God the Father is, of course, more familiar to us than God the *Pantocrator*. God's fatherhood
has been given a great deal of attention in recent years.
As all feminist theologians rightly insist, the metaphor

"father" needs constantly to be supplemented by many other metaphors, including that of "friend," which has neither patriarchal nor gender connotations. The assertion that God is Father remains an indispensable part of trinitarian understanding of the creed, nevertheless, because it connotes intimacy, what Otto called the *fascinans*.

God welcomes us, welcomes us home with outstretched arms. Just as in the parable of the Prodigal Son, the Father even runs down the road to meet us. God is the one with whom we can be at home, be comfortable, be comforted. This aspect of God's nature was central to Jesus' teaching, of course, and one can learn more about it from the many fine studies of the Aramaic word Jesus used for Father, *Abba*. For our purposes, the important thing to notice is the invitation that title offers us: come closer.

My efforts to explain Otto's technical term *fascinans* have led me to speak of this attractive side of holiness as magnetic. The Holy draws us to itself just as Jesus apparently understood *Abba* to do. No other word better expresses that warm, personal side of holiness than Father, I think, the compassionate and merciful God so prominent in the descriptions that began this chapter.

Otto's term for the other dimension of the Holy is more difficult to put into the vernacular. I frequently use "holy dynamite," but it is not altogether satisfactory. What needs to be conveyed is the idea that one should not come too close. The holy mountain might be radioactive, as it were. One should approach it with something other than ordinary shoes on the feet—or perhaps not even standing upright at all.

A closer look at the term translated "the Almighty" in the Nicene Creed today is in order. It has an interesting history, and its translation from Hebrew to Greek to Latin to English has caused many problems for us in our understanding of the Bible and the Christian tradition.

The Hebrew forerunner of what became *Pantocrator* in the Greek translation of the Hebrew Scripture, the Septuagint or LXX, is *El Shaddai.* Modern English translations render *El Shaddai* as "God Almighty," often with a footnote telling us that such is the traditional meaning of *El Shaddai.* A biblical dictionary may also tell you that it means "the Mountain One." The modern commentary on the newer Jewish translations states in plain words that the original meaning of the term is uncertain, that the traditional rendering has no basis in fact. They chose therefore simply to transliterate the Hebrew. As a result, their Torah makes it clear that the chief name of God in patriarchal times was *El Shaddai* until God revealed the divine name to Moses in Exodus 6:2-3. There God says, "I appeared to Abraham, Isaac and Jacob as God Almighty (*El Shaddai*), but by my name 'the Lord (*Yahweh*),' I did not make myself known to them."

By late New Testament times, Christian readers hearing the Hebrew Scriptures read in Greek were thoroughly accustomed to the Torah's title for God Almighty, *Pantocrator.* It is in that sense that it occurs in the letters of Paul once, in an Old Testament quotation in 2 Corinthians 6:18, which ends, "says the Lord Almighty." Other New Testament occurrences of *Pantocrator* are found only in the Book of Revelation, where it is clearly a title of address to God. In Revelation 4:8 the seraphim unceasingly sing,

> Holy, holy, holy,
> The Lord God the Almighty.

When that title is translated once again into Latin we meet it not as a title but as an attribute. What is God like? Among a whole list of other attributes, God is said to be *omnipotent*. And very shortly this attribute prompts absurd philosophical speculations of the sort people often associate with the kind of medieval theological trivia in the question, "How many angels can stand on the end of a needle?" If God is omnipotent, for example, is God powerful enough to make a stone so heavy that even an all-powerful God cannot lift it? I'm told that similar discussions still occur among college freshmen in late-night dormitory sessions.

Nevertheless, the question of God's omnipotence deserves our serious attention. The idea raises a multitude of questions when tested against our experience. If God is omnipotent, why does God not bring an end to cancer, for example? If God is both almighty *and* a loving father, why is there so much evil in the world? Some responsible theologians conclude that God is limited in power, or is still in the process of becoming. What do you think?

Apparently it is not until the third or fourth century at the earliest that the term *Pantocrator* came to be glued to the term *Pater*, as if we were speaking about one attribute of God instead of two. In the oldest extant text of the Nicene Creed, however, they are clearly two

20

separate ideas of who God is, even as in our newer version.

By the time we have recited all three paragraphs of the creed, we have added to the idea of who God is. We affirm that this one God is also God the Son and God the Holy Spirit. What kind of sense does that make, if any?

The assertion that God is one God in three persons is, to say the least, confusing. One does not find it clearly stated in the New Testament, although in at least two places it is surely implicit. In Matthew's gospel Jesus tells his disciples to go baptize in the name of the Father and the Son and the Holy Spirit (28:19), and at the end of Paul's second letter to the Corinthians he uses the doxology, "The grace of the Lord Jesus Christ, and the love of God, and the fellowship of the Holy Spirit be with you all" (13:14). Nevertheless, the full-blown doctrine of the Trinity is the product of several centuries of reflection on the meaning of Christian experience.

Understanding the distortions caused by translation can help clear up some of the problems in understanding this doctrine. Although it does not eliminate them, it does make it sound a little less like nonsense to say that Christians believe in one God in three "persons." We may still think, as an old paraphrase of the Athanasian Creed put it, that we are asked to believe in a Father incomprehensible, a Son incomprehensible, a Holy Spirit incomprehensible, the whole thing incomprehensible. Nevertheless we will then be confronted by genuine Mystery rather than unnecessary mystification.

Let's begin with the fact that the Greeks enjoyed philosophy and that they had developed a sophisticated philosophical vocabulary. They liked to discuss such metaphysical questions as "What is the nature of Being?" From the time of Plato to the fourth century A.D., the Greeks were intrigued by the relationship of the One and the Many. Not only professional philosophers but also ordinary men and women took an interest in such things, judging from contemporary writings.

The Romans, on the other hand, were of a far less speculative turn of mind. They liked law—as well as order. Since the doctrine of the Trinity was developed by Greek theologians, using their richly endowed and polished philosophical vocabulary, they were able to affirm subtle nuances of meaning for which Latin had no precise equivalent. Most especially, the Greeks had one term for Being itself (*ousia*) and another term for Being as differentiated (*hypostasis*). Both words meant something very close to the same thing.

The North African theologian Tertullian, writing at the beginning of the third century, has been called the father of Latin theology since he is the first person, as far as we know, to attempt to write about the triune being of God in that language. Since there was no Latin cognate for *ousia* (Being itself), he chose a very plausible Latin word as equivalent. God was one *substantia*, one underlying reality. Of course. Yet, alas, *substantia* literally means "that which stands under," which is the literal meaning of *hypostasis* as well.

Since the Latin vocabulary of Being was now exhausted, Tertullian drew on terminology from the contemporary drama (and the law courts) to serve the purpose. Even as one actor can wear three different masks on stage and thus be said to be three *personae*, so with God. God is one *substantia* in three *personae*. We still use that term for the cast of characters in a play, one of Shakespeare's, perhaps. We encounter a list of *dramatis personae*.

By now you can see what happens when we move into English, especially modern English, which bears witness to major philosophical, psychological, and theatrical changes. Instead of one *ousia* in three *hypostases*, or even one *substantia* in three *personae*, we are asked to believe in one *substance* in three *persons*. That is a one-hundred-and-eighty degree change. To any English speaker, substance is that which is most solid and unchanging about anything, in spite of Einstein, while person suggests a distinct personality—someone who cannot be duplicated, someone who is unique. That is about as far as anyone could get from what the Greeks were talking about. Tragic, yes—but perhaps to realize this is some help in understanding our difficulties with the idea of a triune God.

When one starts to think about the doctrine of the Trinity one has to start either with the oneness or with the threeness. It is impossible to start at both ends at once. Some people begin with a thought about God's oneness and go on to think about God's trifold character as Christians experience it. Others start with God's three-in-oneness and move toward emphasis on God's unity. The former direction of thought was typical of western theologians and the latter more typical of Greek theologians, judging from the great ancient treatises on the Trinity. The best examples of the two approaches are perhaps Gregory of Nyssa's essay, "One Not Three Gods," written about 375, and Augustine's justly acclaimed *De Trinitate*, written over a period of twenty years, from 399 to 419. Augustine was not a slow writer; he was just a terribly busy bishop.

Gregory is one of those three leading bishops collectively called the Cappadocian Fathers—Cappadocia is a province in what is now Turkey—although historians increasingly recognize that Gregory's older sister, Macrina, was a theologian of equal competence. The other two are Basil the Great, Gregory's brother, and Gregory of Nazianzus, his friend and fellow student at the university in Athens. Gregory of Nyssa wrote his short treatise in response to a question posed to him by another church scholar, who asked why we don't acknowledge three gods when we talk of God the Father, God the Son, and God the Holy Spirit. The theologian's answer hinged on the Platonic concept of the Idea, which refers to a reality prior to any embodiments of that reality in particular individuals. Using the illustration of three men, Peter, James, and John, Gregory argued that the three share one common nature, human nature. It is the same with God: Father, Son, and Spirit share one divine reality, one Godhead.

Gregory's illustration has led to charges of "tritheism" by critics; indeed it would be, without the Platonic presupposition it rests on. An equivalent of the Peter, James, and John argument is still cherished in Eastern Orthodox piety, moreover. At the World Council of Churches Assembly in Vancouver in 1983, William H. Lazareth of the Faith and Order Secretariat led a moving meditation on God the Trinity. He projected on a giant screen in front of the thousands of delegates a slide of a famous icon by the fifteenth-century Russian Orthodox monk, Andrei Rublev. The icon depicts the triune God through the image of three holy men sitting around a table on which rests a chalice. The icon is based on a story in Genesis 18 of God's self-revelation to Abraham through a visitation from three men, a story that begins, "And the Lord appeared to him by the oaks of Mamre" (Gen. 18:1).

In Orthodox thought an icon is a kind of window into heaven. In his meditation, Lazareth emphasized that this particular icon reveals God as a community of love, as "Perfect Unity in Community," in the exchange of love among Father, Son, and Spirit, a love shared with humanity through the Eucharist. That is the ground for the Orthodox use of social analogies for the Trinity.

Western theologians tend to stress the unity of God, using analogies based on individual human beings. Such was the case at least with Augustine's efforts to explain the Trinity, especially to himself. He experiments with a number of triads in his own experience, such as that of mind, its knowledge and its love, or of memory, understanding, and will. A mental trinity satisfies him most fully. Finally Augustine examines the possibility of wisdom, its knowledge of itself and its love of itself, for the adequacy of that analogy. At the heart of all this reflection (fifteen so-called books, which even the author admits is a long discourse on the subject) is the notion that we are made in God's image, hence self-reflection can lead to contemplation of God's unity and God's diversity, and to our love of that God.

An Augustinian approach to thinking about the Trinity is also well represented among modern theologians. Dorothy L. Sayers's *The Mind of the Maker* is a good example. Reflecting on her own experience as a creative writer, she explores the Idea in the writer's mind, its incarnation in words on a written page, and its communication to the reader. It is an effective analogy, but it seems to me a bit coldly intellectual in comparison with Lazareth's theological meditation on the Rublev icon. Even if the eastern approach risks the charge of tritheism, it seems to me more capable of speaking convincingly of God's outgoing love.

In this chapter we have sketched an answer to two dimensions of the question "Who is God?" We have seen that the creed insists on God's oneness while presupposing God's triune nature. We have seen that the creed does not declare faith in an almighty Father but in a God who is at once Father and *Pantocrator*, intimate and awesome, immanent and transcendent. This God is Holy Being.

Chapter 3

Who is Creator?

Maker of heaven and earth,
of all that is, seen and unseen.

C reation made the front page of the newspaper
some time ago with headlines announcing new
findings supporting the theory of the "Big
Bang," the theory that the universe came into being all
at once in a gigantic explosion rather than gradually
over time. The *Washington Post* was prompted to print
an editorial on the event, concluding that the new evidence implies that the universe is "an even weirder
place" than direct observation suggests. Quoting a University of California physicist, *Newsweek* captioned their
report on the new discovery "The Handwriting of
God."

The Big Bang theory and other scientific developments in the last half of the twentieth century have
raised a host of new questions about the Christian doctrine of creation. Among these developments are dis-
coveries supporting the theory of evolution and a new
sense that we are on the brink of environmental disaster

on this fragile planet and so must rethink our role as its stewards, not its "lords." Because of battles surrounding both of these cultural crises, Christians have had to re-examine biblical and creedal ideas of what it means to say that God is "maker of heaven and earth, of all that is, seen and unseen."

We have come a long way from the notion put forth by Archbishop James Ussher in 1650 that the universe was created in the year 4004. Ussher had a great sense of the sweep of history in the Old Testament. His date for the beginning of the universe was printed at the top of the first page of Genesis in editions of the King James Version of the Bible throughout the next two centuries. Ussher, who was a renowned biblical scholar as well as Archbishop of Armagh and primate of all Ireland, did not stop with the year of creation; he decided the earth came into being at 8 a.m. on October 22, 4004.

Geologists nowadays tell us that the earth has lived four and a half times a thousand million years, an estimate that is as unimaginable to most of us as the magnitude of the national debt. But it is not only the natural sciences that have made us question old assumptions about the created order. The biological sciences have had an equally great impact on ideas of creation. Reverberations from Charles Darwin's 1859 work, *Origin of Species*, are with us still. Historical perspective is helpful in keeping us from jumping aboard the latest ecological bandwagon.

When a high school biology teacher, John Scopes, taught the theory of evolution in Tennessee in 1925, he was arrested and tried for breaking the state law. His trial attracted some of the greatest lawyers and journalists of the day, and raised fundamental questions. How could human beings be descended from the apes? Doesn't the Bible say that God created human beings as a distinct act—and as deliberately as a potter or sculptor brings a particular object into being?

To the psalmist's ancient question of God, "What are human beings that you are mindful of them?" many Christians still reply that God made them a little lower than the angels, not just a little higher than the monkeys. The battle between science and so-called "creationism" continued to be front-page news into the eighties. The television evangelist Jerry Falwell sponsored a televised public debate on the subject in which a protein chemist from the University of California lost to an opposing scientist who said that "God created the universe by special processes not operating today." Politics also play a role in the creation debate, of course, as with the state legislature of Arkansas pressuring textbook publishers to print a copy of Michelangelo's *The Creation of Adam* opposite a sketch of Java man, giving equal time and space to both theories.

In recent years, however, growing awareness of nuclear and other ecological threats to continued human existence are refocusing ideas of God the creator. It is noteworthy that an acclaimed study by Langdon Gilkey entitled *Maker of Heaven and Earth* and published in 1959 included neither the words "ecology" nor "environment" in the index. That was three years before the publication of Rachel Carson's book *The Silent Spring*, frequently hailed as the beginning of the contemporary environmental movement. Then in December 1966 Lynn White addressed the American Association for the Advancement of Science on the topic, "The Historical Roots of Our Ecological Crisis."

White's address laid the blame for the crisis directly at the door of the church:

> Finally, God created Adam and, as an afterthought, Eve to keep man from being lonely. Man named all the animals, thus establishing his dominance over them. God planned all this explicitly for man's benefit and rule: no item in the physical creation had any purpose save to serve man's purposes....Christianity bears a huge burden of guilt.[1]

However, anyone who is familiar with the Bible can see that White thought Genesis 1 and 2 were one creation myth instead of two, and that those texts contained all the Bible had to say about creation. He was mistaken on both counts, but his address attracted a great deal of attention. It was printed in the magazine *Science* the following year and has been reprinted often since then. White is not alone in making such a charge, however. For example, a city planner named Ian L. McHarg agreed with White, and wrote in his 1971 book, *Design with Nature*:

> The Biblical creation story of the first chapter of Genesis...in its insistence upon dominion and subjugation of nature encourages the most exploitative and destructive instincts in man....Indeed, if one seeks license for those who would increase radioactivity, cre-

ate canals and harbors with atomic bombs, employ poisons without constraint, or give consent to the bulldozer mentality, there could be no better injunction than this text.[2]

McHarg made that claim in the same year that the well-known Anglican theologian, John Macquarrie, became Lady Margaret Professor at Oxford University. He chose as the topic of his inaugural address "Creation and Environment." In direct response to Lynn White's by then well-publicized criticism of Christianity, Macquarrie expressed qualified agreement. "We need to move away from the monarchial model of God," he said, "toward the organic model."

In exploring more fully what that means for the doctrine of creation, first we need to ask what, in fact, the Nicene Creed itself says about the creative activity of God.

Four assertions of the creed bear on the question, "Who creates?" It says first that we believe in one God who is "maker of heaven and earth, of all that is, seen and unseen." But it goes on to say that we believe in God the Son, "through whom all things were made." In the third paragraph it adds that God the Spirit is the Lord and giver of life. And finally the creed ends with, "We look for the resurrection of the dead, and the life of the world to come." To put it briefly, the creed says that creation is past, present, and future. God isn't through yet.

An unfortunate process of assimilation, whereby all the activities of God are assigned to one or another of the *personae* of the Triune Being, has had destructive consequences for the doctrine of creation because it leads us to assume that the Father alone is the creator. That is nonsense. All of God does whatever God does. Nevertheless we are still stuck with the mental picture of a monarchial patriarch in a flowing white beard who stretches out his arm and says, "Let it be." That is our heritage from music and art as well as from biblical misinterpretation of the first chapter of Genesis.

The dangers of this kind of distortion in thinking about creation are offset to some extent by the creed's claim that all things were made "through the Son"—a phrase with its own long and tangled history. We will need to be more precise about it in the next chapter when we explore some of the christological debates of the fourth-century church. For the moment, let us simply look at one strand of that history.

The claim that all things were made through the Word, or Logos, the rational principle in the universe, is explicit in the Prologue to the Fourth Gospel. John 1:3 states, "All things were made through him, and without him was not anything made that was made." The writer is here drawing on a very old Jewish tradition about Wisdom and the role of Wisdom in creation. Originally a tradition about an attribute of God that was active in the creative process, this "wisdom" gradually became personified as a feminine figure, Sophia. In the Book of Proverbs, for example, the poet pictures Wisdom existing "at the first, before the beginning of the earth." Wisdom herself speaks: "When he established the heavens, I was there,...when he marked out the foundations of the earth, then I was beside him, like a master worker; and I was daily his delight" (Prov. 8:22-31).

Recently this centuries-long tradition of a feminine element at work in creation has attracted increasing attention from scholars. In a fascinating book called *Till the Heart Sings*, Old Testament scholar Samuel Terrien explores the Wisdom tradition. One chapter traces the development of the figure of Wisdom from Sophia to Logos, from the feminine to the masculine principle, in the intertestamental period.[3] In Terrien's translation of Ecclesiasticus and the Wisdom of Solomon, Sophia is "lady-artisan of the world" rather than the less graphic "fashioner of all things" (Wis. 7:21-22). Terrien argues that John probably uses the term Logos rather than Sophia, although "clearly presenting Jesus as the incarnation of Sophia," in order to avoid confusion with the vocabulary used in the circles of Gnostic mysticism, already understood as heretical from the Evangelist's point of view.

For whatever reasons, the Sophia tradition was gradually absorbed by the Logos tradition, the feminine by the grammatically masculine Word, and thus helped to reinforce the masculine emphasis of early Christian thought. Current efforts to redress the balance take different tacks. One direction is toward identifying the Holy Spirit as a feminine figure. Is she the real heir of Sophia?

Whether or not the Spirit derives from the feminine figure of Wisdom, there is no doubt that God the Spirit is portrayed as a creative God in the creed. The picture that the creationists wanted printed in biology textbooks, the well-known figure from Michelangelo's Sistine Chapel ceiling fresco of God stretching out a finger to the reclining Adam, had always appeared to me to be the quintessential image of God the Father—until I learned more about it. My whole idea of Michelangelo's achievement in the Sistine ceiling was revolutionized by the insights of art historian John Cook, presented in a paper he gave entitled "Images of Creation" at Yale Divinity School.[4]

Unveiled in 1512, Michelangelo's fresco consists of many scenes from Genesis, not only the creation story. That story is almost certainly the best known, however, and usually the spotlight focuses on the creation panels, especially the detail from *The Creation of Adam* in which one can almost see the spark of life leaping from God's hand to awaken the limp hand of Adam. With his artist's eye, Cook played the spotlight over all the panels and argued convincingly that what Michelangelo has given us is a powerful, dynamic portrayal not of God the Father, but God the Spirit. The recently completed cleaning of the Sistine ceiling gives us a clearer picture of the panels than we have had in five hundred years, and it comes as something of a shock now to see that the Creator God is dressed in what appears to be a pink nightgown.

Cook's argument becomes even more compelling, however, when one remembers that at the election of a new Pope to this day, the College of Cardinals gathers under that ceiling in the Vatican's chapel and sings the ancient hymn *Veni Creator Spiritus*. Attributed to the ninth-century theologian Rabanus Maurus, the hymn begins (in one modern translation),

> O Holy Spirit, by whose breath,
>> Life rises vibrant out of death;
> Come to create, renew, inspire,
>> Come, kindle in our hearts your fire.[5]

Not only does the hymn remind us that the Holy Spirit is a full partner in creation, but also that creation is an ongoing activity. For many of us, any question about the Bible's teaching about creation leads us immediately to the primordial myths in Genesis 1 and 2. We forget that creation is not just something God did for six days, once upon a time, and then rested forever after. Creation is past, yes, but it is also future—and, most critically, it is now.

In this context it is appropriate to remember that God is not the static, unchanging God of Greek thought. The biblical God is flexible, responsive, creative. Think of the famous announcement of a new creation in Isaiah. The poet-author of those chapters knew full well who "measured the waters in the hollow of his hand and marked off the heavens with a span," but was also on the alert for impending changes, for a new day: "See, the former things have come to pass and new things I now declare" (Is. 40:12; 42:9). People will be empowered to sing a new song to the Lord, who tells them, "I am about to create new heavens and a new earth" (65:17).

The promise of a renewed creation, a changed situation, which resounds in Isaiah lies behind the claim in our creed that Christ will come again, that we look for

the life of the world to come. Christian faith still antici-
pates a new heaven and a new earth. It is not a cyclical
faith, one that expects a return to some Golden Age of
the past. It is a historical faith, oriented toward the horizon of the future. To think of God as creator is to
think of ever new possibilities because God is daily engaged in new creation.

So are we. Human beings are by nature creative beings. Both Genesis creation myths suggest that we are
made to be co-creators with a creative God. According
to many interpreters, that is what it means, or at least
part of what it means, to say that women and men are
made in the image of God. Genesis 2 puts the same idea
in more concrete language. The new creatures are put
into the garden to tend it. Yahweh brings all the new
animals to Adam to find out what they are to be named.
In Hebrew thought, naming has a performative function. It helps make something whatever it is.

This dimension of our Christian doctrine of creation
is getting renewed attention in this era of environmental awareness. In response to the new situation
there is widespread interest in rebuilding the Christian
creation tradition, which has been obscured by too
strong an emphasis on the salvation of individual human beings. Renewed focus on human co-creativity
seeks to avoid either the passive resignation of Protestant pietism or the opposite extreme that says, "It is all
up to us"—we must build the kingdom of God all by
ourselves.

Some insight into our roles as co-creators seems to
me to come from two very familiar visions of the future

36

in the Bible. The first is Isaiah's prophecy of the new day in Isaiah 11:6-9, and the second is the future of the heavenly city, the new Jerusalem, pictured in Revelation 21:1–22:5.

Familiarity with Isaiah's vision comes to many of us through the work of the nineteenth-century Quaker painter Edward Hicks. His more than fifty paintings depicting *The Peaceable Kingdom* show the restored nature Isaiah speaks of. The lion does indeed lie down with the lamb, as many Christmas cards show us, although in Isaiah's original vision it was the wolf with the lamb, the leopard with the kid, the calf and the lion, the cow and the bear. In that kingdom, in fact, each pair of animals contains one wild and one domesticated animal. It is a vision that will come about, apparently, through human co-creativity with God. Isaiah's oracle ends:

> They will not hurt or destroy
>   on all my holy mountain;
> for the earth will be full of
>   the knowledge of the Lord
> as the waters cover the sea.

The vision of the city of God at the end of the Bible is, of course, an apocalyptic one, but it seems also to suggest in some of its imagery a role for human creativity. This is not a return to Eden, although it is a garden city, to be sure, with a river running through it between leafy banks. Cities are places where people live together. They are conceived and built by artisans. This one is built out of precious stones, with golden streets and gates of pearl. Its gates are never closed. The nations are to come in and walk in the light of the Lord God.

Nature and history are blended in this vision of the future. Creation has not been allowed to remain unaltered by human beings, but is enhanced. Such pictures as those given us by Isaiah and the Seer of the Apocalypse can help save us from romanticism about nature, as well as panic in the face of the possibility of the end of nature. They can help us rescue St. Francis from the bird bath, to borrow a Franciscan's suggestive phrase, so that we may get on with our job of co-creation.

A modern hymn by Catherine Cameron puts the matter in fine balance. Cameron writes:

> God, who stretched the spangled heavens
>   infinite in time and place,
> flung the suns in burning radiance through
>   the silent fields of space:
> we your children in your likeness, share
>   inventive powers with you;
> Great Creator, still creating, show us
>   what we yet may do.[6]

Not only does Cameron's hymn underline our co-creativity, it also reminds us of the phrase in the first paragraph of the Nicene Creed that we have not yet explored, that God is creator "of all that is, seen and unseen." That comma is almost as important, in my opinion, as the comma between "the Father" and "the Almighty." The phrase includes the spiritual realm as well as the material, seen as well as unseen galaxies. God makes all that is. And according to Genesis, God sees that it is very good.

These phrases from Christian tradition have two implications for us. One is that matter and spirit, the seen and the unseen, are both good. The doctrine of creation rules out all dualisms, including the old Gnostic idea that spirit is good but matter is bad, evil. We are not souls imprisoned in bodies that we will eventually escape, but embodied selves.

The second implication of these words is that the material is the vehicle through which the Spirit works. In short, as Archbishop William Temple said so powerfully, we live in a "sacramental universe." He was talking not just about those rites commonly called sacraments, but about sex and dishwashing and gardening and handshakes—about all that is, seen and unseen.

Endnotes

1. Lynn White, "The Historical Roots of Our Ecological Crisis," *Science* (March 1967), pp. 24, 28.

2. Ian L. McHarg, *Design with Nature* (New York: Doubleday, 1971), p. 26.

3. Samuel Terrien, *Till the Heart Sings: A Biblical Theology of Manhood and Womanhood* (Philadelphia: Fortress Press, 1985), pp. 103-120.

4. John W. Cook, "Images of Creation," in *Creation: The Arena of the Divine Drama*, papers from the Symposium at Yale University, April 29-30, 1979, sponsored by the Religion and Arts Program at the Divinity School and the Institute of Sacred Music, pp. 6-13.

5. The Hymnal 1982, 501.

6. The Hymnal 1982, 580.

Chapter 4

Who is the Christ?

We believe in one Lord, Jesus Christ,
the only Son of God,
eternally begotten of the Father,
God from God, Light from Light,
true God from true God,
begotten, not made,
of one Being with the Father.
Through him all things were made.

The second paragraph of the Nicene Creed is the longest of the three because it deals with the question that caused the emperor Constantine to call the Council of Nicea in the first place: Is the Christ really and truly Son of God, or is he some lesser being, an intermediary between God and humanity?

The question is still important to us today because all of us must answer it for ourselves. Jesus of Nazareth himself asks it of us: "What do you think of the Christ?"

(Mt. 22:42). Or again, "But who do you say that I am?" (Mt. 6:14).

When we try to articulate our answers to these questions today, however, we do not think in terms of essence, substance, and nature as they did at the Council of Nicea. Those were the philosophical categories of the debate at that time, but not today. Archbishop William Temple acknowledged the failure of all attempts to explain the Incarnation in those terms as long ago as 1924. Nowadays we are more likely to think in dynamic terms, in categories of doing rather than being, as well as in relational terms. Was God doing something unique in the birth, life, death, and resurrection of Jesus of Nazareth? How was Jesus related to God?

The answer that the ecumenical church arrived at in 325 was amplified over the next century and a quarter to produce, by 451, what is known as "The Chalcedonian Definition of the Union of the Divine and Human Natures in the Person of Christ." The statement is now printed among the historical documents at the back of the Book of Common Prayer. It asserts that our Lord Jesus Christ is one hundred percent God and one hundred percent human, the two natures coming together to form one Person, "without confusion, without change, without division, without separation." This language was not ever used in the Nicene Creed itself, but its affirmations are all implicit there, as the council claimed when they began their statement, "Therefore, following the holy fathers, we all with one accord teach...." Yes, the Christ was fully God. Yes, he was fully human. But he was one Person, not a schizo-phrenic.

The debates about the person of the Christ which led up to the first four ecumenical conferences were occasioned by what Bishop J. W. C. Wand has called "the four great heresies"—those of Arius, Apollinaris, Nestorius, and Eutyches. Each of these churchmen wrestled with a formulation of the christological question that arose logically out of the previous answer.

Arius, the first of them, we have already learned about in Chapter 1. Arius was concerned lest the unity of the one God be somehow compromised, so he claimed that the Logos or Word of God was not co-eternal with the Father, but a lesser being, created by God. Arius was willing to say that the Logos was the first of God's creatures; he was too canny to insist that there was a *time* when the Logos was not, since that would mean the Logos was created after God created time. A favorite text of the Arians came from the eighth chapter of Proverbs: "The Lord created me at the beginning of his work, the first of his acts of long ago" (8:22).

Arius's chief opponent and spokesman for the Nicene faith was Athanasius. He was a deacon in 325, at the time of the first council, and he became Bishop of Alexandria shortly thereafter and spent a lifetime defending the position of that council. From his point of view, the issue was salvation. Only God could save fallen humanity. If, therefore, Jesus Christ is Savior, the Christ must be God. Athanasius found great support in the text of John 1: "In the beginning was the Word, and the Word was with God, and the Word was God." This was the one, Athanasius and his party said, who acted for our salvation, becoming incarnate in the person of Jesus.

The next question to capture the attention of the church followed naturally from the Nicene decision that the Christ is fully God. If so, can he also be fully human? The great "heretic" who came up with a qualified "no" to this question was a third churchman, Apollinaris, a bishop of Laodicea. Apollinaris was a good theologian, with a sophisticated anthropology. Presupposing a tripartite selfhood in any human being, consisting of a body, an animal soul, and a rational soul—the mind or *nous*—Apollinaris concluded that Jesus was fully human in respect to his body and his animal soul, but his mind was the mind of God.

At the Council of Constantinople in 381, Apollinaris was judged to be heretical on the grounds that he was really saying that Jesus is only two-thirds human. Again, the heart of the matter in the eyes of the majority was the issue of our salvation: if the Son of God did not assume all of human nature, he could not redeem it. His identification with humanity had to be complete.

The next two christological questions are not as clearcut, and the councils that dealt with them were far more obviously plagued by political factions and regional quarrels. At the Council of Ephesus in 431, the issue on the agenda was the unity of the person of Jesus Christ. Was he really one person or was he split between two natures, as it were, both Son of God and Son of Man?

A new bishop in the city of Constantinople, one Nestorius by name, brought this question to the forefront.

Nestorius came to his new diocese from Antioch. Before he had been there long enough to question the liturgical customs in his new see, he raised questions about the use in worship of a word identifying the Virgin Mary. She was called *theotokos*, God-bearer. In Nestorius's mind, that title gave Mary far more honor than she was entitled to. He preferred to call Mary merely Christ-bearer, mother of the Messiah. In the ensuing debate, Nestorius was accused of saying, in effect, that Jesus Christ was ultimately two persons, two sons, although there is reason today to believe that he never actually said any such thing. This later judgment is based on the late nineteenth-century discovery of lost writings by Nestorius, found dramatically and accidentally in a bazaar in Syria.

The last of the great christological councils was that of Chalcedon in 451, which adopted the definition ratifying the position of the previous councils and came up with its own answer to the then-current form of the question. It was posed by an aged monk named Eutyches, whom modern historians describe as at best "muddle-headed." Eutyches firmly believed that Christ was not one Person with two "natures," one human and one divine, but that he had only one "nature," a divine-human one. The issue this time was beclouded by the fact that Eutyches had imperial clout; he was godfather to one or more of the palace children, and when he was summoned before the council he came escorted by an imperial guard. Eutyches was judged heretical, nevertheless. Chalcedon insisted on two natures—joined in one Person without mixture or confusion. That many

44

eastern Christians disagreed is evident from the existence of the Coptic and Armenian churches, both monophysite in theology, teaching one nature—one *physis*—only.

The Chalcedonian definition poses several major problems for a modern Christian. Most serious is that there really is no such discrete entity as a human nature or a divine nature, something that is presupposed in the ancient debate. Still less can these two natures be compared on the same level.

Closely related to that is the lack of dynamism in the language used in the Chalcedonian definition. It is a static statement that gives us a Greek God, far from the passionate Hebraic God who is active in biblical revelation. The Greek idea of deity is expressed in the first of the Thirty-Nine Articles of Religion: God is "without body, parts, and passions." The biblical God, on the other hand, brings the Israelites out of Egypt with "a mighty arm and outstretched hand." The biblical God can show fierce anger and compassionate tenderness. Abraham can even persuade such a God to change an intended course of action against Sodom.

The God of Chalcedon lacks poetry, as the New Testament scholar Amos Wilder put it. Theology is "theopoetic," he insisted. "It does not permit of merely abstract, wooden, or pedantic treatment....It must assert the rights of the imagination against abstraction, rationalism, and stereotype."[1]

What, then, does a Christian today do with the definition reached by the Council of Chalcedon? Scrap it completely? Reaffirm it without question? Or give it a qualified reaffirmation, accepting it as outlining the christological questions with which all thoughtful persons must somehow deal in their own terms, using their own categories? As one contemporary theologian put it, "We can't live with it and we can't live without it."

One of the difficulties in thinking about the person of Jesus Christ is, of course, that one has to start thinking somewhere, a difficulty similar to that of the trinitarian dilemma. In the case of the Christ, one has to start either with God or with Jesus; one must do Christology either "from above" or "from below," as the problem has been phrased by contemporary theologians such as Wolfhart Pannenberg and John A. T. Robinson.

The differences in starting points are already evident in the New Testament period; Paul's letter to the Romans offers a fine example of doing Christology "from below." In the opening salutation, Paul speaks of Jesus Christ "who was descended from David according to the flesh and was declared to be Son of God with power according to the spirit of holiness by resurrection from the dead" (1:3-4). Clearly, if this idea were pushed to the limit, it would lead to adoptionism, the position that God adopted the man Jesus at some point in his life, such as at his baptism or at the resurrection. This is close to what someone once caricatured as the "Christianity of Main Street," as a log-cabin-to-White-House story.

The real gospel is a story that moves from Buckingham Palace to the slums of London. That is the direction taken in the Prologue of John's gospel, which states that the Word was made flesh, and also in what was probably an ancient hymn in Paul's letter to the Philippians, a hymn that begins,

> Let the same mind be in you that was in Christ Jesus, who, though he was in the form of God, did not regard equality with God as something to be exploited, but emptied himself, taking the form of a slave, being born in human likeness. (2:5-7)

Such a formulation poses its own dangers. Pushed to its extreme, it leads to the position that Jesus only seemed to be human; he wasn't really so. Technically this is a heresy called docetism, named after the Greek word *dokein*, meaning "to appear or seem." Since it is impossible for any one person to avoid all the pitfalls in thinking about Jesus Christ, it seems to me that docetism is by far and away the greatest danger to healthy faith today. Although the creed begins its christological paragraph "from above," the one who came down from heaven was emphatically "made man." Jesus was a first-century Palestinian Jew with all the limitations of his time and place. He spent nine months in the womb of a young country girl, he was tortured to death by the Roman government, and he truly died and was buried. None of this was a divine charade.

We are left with two major questions about Jesus Christ in paragraph two of the Nicene Creed, the question of his conception and of his resurrection and ascension. We will discuss what salvation might mean in the next chapter and reserve the question of his so-called Second Coming for a penultimate chapter on eschatology, or "last things."

First, what do we mean when we say, "by the power of the Holy Spirit he became incarnate from the Virgin Mary?" The question causes a lot of distress, in my judgment, when literalists confront mythic or figurative language. Over a decade ago such a confrontation occurred when the theologians of Oxford University published a book called *The Myth of God Incarnate*. The book had barely reached the bookstores when a group of Cambridge theologians rushed into print with an angry rejoinder they called *The Truth of God Incarnate*. That title clearly reflects a gross misunderstanding of the term "myth" as theologians and historians of religion use the word. It does not mean something untrue, something contrary to fact, like the tale of the Tooth Fairy. Instead, mythic thinking conveys truth in narrative form. The assertion in the creed that "he became incarnate from the Virgin Mary" is a theological, not a biological, statement. The language once again is mythopoetic if not altogether mythic. I prefer Amos Wilder's term, "theopoetic." It is asserting that the initiative in Mary's conception of Jesus came from God, but not how God exercised that initiative other than "by the power of the Holy Spirit."

Reputable and devout theologians share this interpretation of the virginal conception. In his book, *God Who Dares To Be Man*, Bonnell Spencer argued that based on what we now know about genetics, parthenogenesis would necessarily have produced a female child.[2] As any reader of the Bible knows, the legend of a virginal conception appears only in the gospels of Matthew and

Luke. It is not mentioned at all by Paul or by the earliest of the evangelists, Mark.

The birth narratives given to us in Matthew and Luke, furthermore, differ widely. Luke has the story of an annunciation by the angel Gabriel and those shepherds watching over their flocks by night. Matthew also has an annunciation, but it is to Joseph in a dream, and wise men following a star from the East. (He never says there were three of them.) Christmas wouldn't seem like Christmas without these beloved narratives, but the truth of the Incarnation does not rest on their veracity. Both are serving the theological purposes of their respective evangelists. The doctrine of the virginal conception of Jesus serves the theological purpose of asserting that God acted uniquely in history in the conception of the man Jesus. The only agency mentioned is "the power of the Holy Spirit," and one could rightly claim that any conception is by the same power. The Spirit is, as the creed itself asserts, "the Lord, the giver of life."

Something similar must be said about the resurrection and ascension. Perhaps the easiest way to put it, however crude a statement, is that neither event could have been subject to video-taping had someone been there with a camcorder. The Easter narratives without exception stress both the Risen Lord's continuity and his discontinuity with the earthly Jesus his friends had known. Usually they don't recognize him when he appears, until he speaks to them.

He walks through closed and locked doors, but urges them to feel the wounds in his hand. Mary Magdalen mistakes him for a gardener until he calls her by name. He cooks a beach breakfast picnic for some weary fishermen like Peter, but first he miraculously helps them fill a net full of fish. On the road to Emmaus he talks to two disciples during a seven-mile hike, expounding Scripture, but he only becomes known to them "in the breaking of the bread" after they invite this apparent stranger to supper. This was no resuscitation of a corpse. Jesus was the same, but different.

All of these narratives have come to us honed by years of oral tradition, of telling and retelling, almost certainly in the context of eucharistic worship. The strongest evidence for the resurrection of Jesus for many Christians is not an empty tomb, but the startling transformation of a scattered bunch of frightened friends of the executed man. Almost within a month they were revitalized, fearless, vigorously proclaiming the good news that God had raised Jesus from the dead. As Peter puts it in the book of Acts in his speech to the people of Jerusalem, "God raised him up, having freed him from death, because it was impossible for him to be held in its power" (Acts 2:24). Paul says something comparable in his efforts to explain the resurrection to the people in the church at Corinth. "If Christ has not been raised," he argues, "your faith is futile" (1 Cor. 15:17). But then Paul goes on to say of the resurrection of all the baptized, "It is sown a physical body, it is raised a spiritual body" (15:44). He compares it to the difference between a bare kernel of wheat sown in the ground and the new life that springs from it.

By the same token, had you been present on what Christians call Ascension Day, you could not have photographed Jesus going up into the clouds, not even the soles of his feet. Luke is the only one to describe it, and what he has to say is that Jesus' disciples saw him lifted up "and a cloud took him out of their sight" (Acts 1:9). In mythopoetic language the creed is saying that the Risen Lord is with God the Father.

An often ignored corollary of this statement is that the Incarnation had a beginning, but it has not ended. It was Jesus of Nazareth, the incarnate Logos, who was resurrected and who ascended. Humanity is bonded to divinity for all time. The God-Man, in the words of the Letter to the Hebrews, "ever liveth to make intercession for us," his sisters and brothers.

Endnotes

1. Amos Niven Wilder, *Theopoetic: Theology and the Religious Imagination* (Philadelphia: Fortress Press, 1976), p. 57.

2. Bonnell Spencer, *God Who Dares To Be Man: Theology for Prayer and Suffering* (New York: The Seabury Press, 1980), p. 93.

Chapter 5

What is Salvation?

For us and for our salvation he came down
from heaven: by the power of the Holy Spirit
he became incarnate from the Virgin Mary,
and was made man.
For our sake he was crucified under Pontius
Pilate; he suffered death and was buried.
On the third day he rose again in accordance
with the Scriptures; he ascended into heaven
and is seated at the right hand of the Father.
He will come again in glory to judge the living
and the dead, and his kingdom will have no end.

This crucial phrase in the second paragraph of the creed, "For us and for our salvation," deserves a whole chapter to itself. "Salvation" is one of those words that has lost meaning for most of us. There is no great public demand for such a commodity. Even though the root meaning of salvation is "health" or "wholeness," its religious equivalent is out of style. Indeed it brings to mind wild-eyed fanatics who button-hole people to ask, "Sister, are you saved?" Perhaps a better way of putting the question before us is, "What was it that God did for the human family through Jesus Christ?"

Whatever metaphors we use to describe the experience, Christians are in general agreement that in Christ's incarnation, his life, death, and resurrection, God established a new relationship with human beings. The traditional word used to talk about this new relationship is "atonement," which probably meant "to cover" in the original Hebrew, in the sense of "covering sin." Traditionally theologians have discussed the atonement under the rubric "The Work of Christ"; just as the creed insists, Jesus Christ did something for us.

One of the curious facts in the history of Christian thought is that the church has never attempted to define officially how the death of one man could accomplish anything approaching an at-one-ment—a useful if illegitimate breakdown of the word—that is effective for everyone, everywhere, forever. The many attempts to do so have ranged all the way from the magnificent exposition in Paul's letter to the Romans to Gregory of Nyssa's bizarre claim that God baited a trap for the devil with God's own son.

In the Pauline view, a key metaphor for the work of Christ is the gift of freedom. In his letter to the Galatians, Paul put it succinctly, "For freedom Christ has set us free" (5:1). In his longer and more systematic development of the theme in his letter to the Romans, this new freedom is threefold. Through the act of God in Christ, we are free from sin, free from death, free from the law. And by "law" Paul did not mean just the Jewish law, the Torah, but the very principle of law. No obedience to any set of rules, including the Ten Commandments, is the way to gain genuine freedom. It is almost easier to accept the idea of freedom from sin and death for American Christians than from law, because we really believe that by earnest effort we can earn God's approval and a place in heaven for ourselves. What we can hardly believe is that God's love for us is not contingent on good behavior.

Paul's formulation of the work of Christ in terms of freedom is not the only interpretation in the New Testament, although it has probably played the most significant role in the church over the centuries, especially because of its place in the thought of Augustine of Hippo and Martin Luther. The biblical writers, including Paul, had a variety of other ways of speaking about the atonement and about the experience of salvation. At least three of these—victory, ransom, and sacrifice—demand elaboration because they have been so influential.

First we can explore the metaphors of battle and conquest. Not far below the surface in such metaphors is the idea of a cosmic battle, a war between good and evil, between God and the devil—a battle that includes not only human beings, but angelic powers. What has Christ accomplished? In the language of Colossians, "he disarmed the rulers and authorities and made a public example of them, triumphing over them" (2:15). Or in an even better-known passage in Paul's first letter to the Corinthians:

> "Death has been swallowed up in victory."
> "Where, O death, is your victory?
>   Where, O death, is your sting?"
> The sting of death is sin, and the power of sin is the law. But thanks be to God, who gives us the victory through our Lord Jesus Christ. (1 Cor. 15:54b-56)

That triad of sin, death, and the law is the same that Paul used in Romans, but only here does he say that Christ has won a victory over them. The quotations from Scripture at the beginning of that paragraph depend loosely on similar statements and questions in the prophets Isaiah and Hosea. Isaiah claims that God "will swallow up death forever" (25:7) and Hosea asks, "O Death, where are your plagues? O Sheol, where is your destruction?" (13:14).

In a little book called *Christus Victor* published some years ago, the Swedish theologian Gustav Aulen called this the "classic" theory of the atonement. He thought it was the dominant one in the writings of many of the church fathers, most notably the second-century apologist Irenaeus, a Gallic bishop. The victory theme still rings out loudly every Easter in the parish churches where people sing a seventeenth-century Latin hymn:

> The strife is o'er, the battle done,
>   the victory of life is won;
> The song of triumph has begun.
>   Alleluia!

> The powers of death have done their worst,
>> but Christ their legions hath dispersed;
> Let shout of holy joy outburst.
>> Alleluia![1]

Nowadays the victory metaphor is less popular than it used to be, however. Many people want to avoid military imagery, and the mythic idea of a cosmic battle is not a congenial one for us. We read more than enough about human wars without projecting them into heavenly realms. The TV screens show so much death that the thought of war in heaven has little or no appeal to us.

A second way of talking about the work of salvation uses the idea of "ransom," an idea expressed directly in Matthew's gospel: "The Son of Man came not to be served but to serve, and to give his life a ransom for many" (20:28). The writer of the letter to Timothy echoes that idea but with a difference when speaking of the man Christ Jesus "who gave himself a ransom for all" (1 Tim. 2:6). Not just "many," but "all." (We will need to return shortly to the question, for whom did Christ die?) In the Mediterranean world, ransoms were given to redeem slaves and prisoners of war; we know it today from kidnapping and hostage-taking. But to whom was Christ paying ransom? The New Testament does not say.

Gregory of Nyssa, one of the fourth-century Cappadocian Fathers we met when exploring the doctrine of the Trinity, is the author of the so-called "fishhook" theory of the atonement. God paid a ransom to the devil and thereby tricked him of his hold over humanity.

In Gregory's mind, this method was consonant with God's justice and God's wisdom: "In order to secure that the ransom on our behalf might easily be accepted by him who required it, the Deity was hidden under the veil of our nature that so, as with the ravenous fish, the hook of Deity might be gulped down with the bait of flesh."[2]

One doesn't know whether to laugh or shudder at this idea of God using God's Son to trick the devil, yet a version of it still appears in a much-loved Holy Week hymn by Fortunatus.

> The royal banners forward go,
>   the cross shines forth in mystic glow,
> where he through whom our flesh was made,
>   in that same flesh our ransom paid.

The hymn goes on to speak of

> the price which none but he could pay
>   to spoil the spoiler of his prey.[3]

Some Christians, on the other hand, were certain that the "ransom" was paid to God on behalf of sinful humanity. Another familiar hymn, "There is a green hill far away," adopts this view in the words,

> There was no other good enough
>   to pay the price of sin;
> He only could unlock the gate
>   of heaven and let us in.[4]

Close cousin to the idea behind this hymn is another well-known atonement theory, that of the medieval theologian Anselm of Canterbury. He spells out the so-called "satisfaction" theory in his book *Cur Deus Homo* or *Why a God-Man?* in the form of a dialogue with a man named Boso. Anselm comes up with an atonement theory that makes use of the feudal metaphors of his own age: humanity has offended God's honor by failing to pay full liege loyalty to their Lord, just as a vassal offended his feudal lord's honor if he failed to give him full and complete allegiance as the law commanded. Only a God-man could vindicate God's violated honor.

Satisfaction language lingers still in some eucharistic liturgies, as does the language of sacrifice, the third biblical metaphor I have chosen for emphasis. The most extensive biblical elaboration of sacrificial terminology is found in the Letter to the Hebrews. There it is said that Christ "has appeared once for all at the end of the age to remove sin by the sacrifice of himself" (9:26). The temple sacrifices on the Day of Atonement had to be repeated year after year, but not so the sacrifice of Christ: "We have been sanctified through the offering of the body of Jesus Christ once for all" (10:10). Christ has offered for all time a single sacrifice for sin. Indeed, in the complex cultic language used in Hebrews as well as elsewhere in the New Testament, Christ is both victim and high priest, both *Agnus Dei*, the lamb of God, and the one who has entered the Holy of Holies, not once a year but for all time.

Sacrificial language finds pride of place in yet another Lenten hymn written by the remarkable medieval scholar, Peter Abelard, a younger contemporary of Anselm. Abelard is one of my favorite question-raisers. He asked one hundred and fifty questions about the Christian faith and answered each of them *Sic et Non*, yes and no, right out of the Bible and the church fathers. Contradiction 116 of *Sic et Non* is a good example: "That the sins of the fathers are passed on to the children, and the contrary." Exodus 20:5 says, "I the Lord your God am a jealous God, punishing children for the iniquity of parents, to the third and fourth generation...," whereas Ezekiel 18:20 claims, "A child shall not suffer for the iniquity of a parent."[5] Abelard believed—rightly, in my opinion—that "by doubting we come to enquiry and by enquiring we perceive the truth."[6]

An Irish medieval scholar, Helen Wadell, wrote a novel about this complicated and controversial theologian and his famous affair with Heloise, one she called simply *Peter Abelard*. She says that Abelard had written for his young students, "challenging them to doubt, arming them against the deadlier sin of dullness."[7] He has been criticized for many of his theological opinions. On the subject of the doctrine of the atonement his critics put him in a pigeon-hole labelled "example theory," the theory that what God did for the human family through Jesus Christ was to provide us with a role model, a good example of a human being. Perhaps. But if this hymn of Abelard's is the source of that label, Jesus' merely exemplary life is far from what he is talking about:

> Alone thou goest forth, O Lord,
>   In sacrifice to die;
> Is this thy sorrow naught to us
>   Who pass unheeding by?

Our sins, not thine, thou bearest, Lord,
  Make us thy sorrow feel,
Till through our pity and our shame
  Love answers love's appeal.[8]

Of all these attempts to make sense out of what Jesus accomplished "for us and for our salvation," the one that is held in the greatest favor today is the Pauline idea of freedom, or its cognate, liberation. Liberation theology has, in fact, dominated the theological scene for some years now. One day in September 1984, the *New York Times* even made it the front-page story. Brazilian theologian Leonardo Boff, author of *Jesus Christ Liberator: A Critical Christology for Our Time*, was summoned to the Vatican for investigation. His book went into a fourth printing of the English translation two months after the Vatican denounced the movement.

How is liberation defined by those who make it the key to their theology? The clearest brief definition I know puts it this way. The theology's goal is "liberation of all men and women from whatever binds them, both internally and externally," surely very close to Paul's idea of freedom if more sweeping in its definition.[9] This statement occurs in the foreword to a collection of writings by Third World women theologians who met in Mexico in 1986 and came from Asia and Africa as well as from Latin America. Since a distinctive feature of liberation theology is its emphasis on speaking from and to one's own life-situation, it is impossible to have liberation theology "in general"—the context is all-important. Some particular contexts that concern liberation theologians are the black experience in America and women's experiences of sexism.

Liberation theologians have refocused the emphasis of salvation ideas. For far too long, too many Christians have thought that salvation was the saving of their own souls. The notion was privatized and individualized. For theologians like Boff and Gustavo Guttierez, however, theology begins with analysis and critique of the social and political ills of the time. Frequently Marxist ideas about class struggle have been used in this phase of the work, which is what so upset the Vatican in the case of Boff. Nevertheless the liberationists insist that Christian faith dictates solidarity with the poor and the oppressed, and so requires commitment to changing the social order.

In practice such theologians work to apply Christian social principles to Third World conditions, trying in a variety of ways to empower the people. They are as much interested in physical as in spiritual hunger, stressing Luke's version of the beatitude, "Blessed are you poor" over Matthew's "Blessed are the poor in spirit." Like the Hebrew prophets before them, they criticize religious institutions; Boff accuses Christians of burying Christ in the churches. Christ belongs in the economic and political spheres of our lives as much, if not more, than in the religious realm. Salvation has to do with the well-being of the whole person.

The perspective of liberation theology helps to sharpen two additional questions about salvation. In a pluralistic age, what are we to make of biblical claims such as "There is salvation in no one else" except Jesus

Christ (Acts 4:12), and "No one comes to the Father except through me" (Jn. 14:6)? And can the crucifixion of one man some two thousand years ago really be the pivot point of all human history? To ask both these questions is a way of raising doubts about what has long been called "the scandal of particularity"—the fact that the Incarnation took place at a particular time and place in history, through one particular human being.

A logo adopted by the World Council of Churches Assembly in Vancouver in 1984 nicely answers the first question. The theme was "Jesus Christ, the Life of the World," and the logo showed a stick-figure Christ hugging a globe to his chest. This is a clear answer also to the question we shelved temporarily earlier in this chapter, "For whom did Christ die?" The answer is, "Everyone." This universalism is similar to that of 1 John, which says that Jesus Christ is "the atoning sacrifice for our sins, and not for ours only but also for the sins of the whole world" (2:2).

Yet the inhabitants of the globe are Muslims, Buddhists, Hindus, Jews, and members of a number of other world religions, as well as not a few complete secularists claiming no religion whatsoever. Not quite two billion human beings out of a world population of over five billion call on the name of Christ. How are they related to the salvation Christ brings?

In a harsh attack on "the scandal of particularity" in his book *Christ in a Changing World*, Tom Driver calls for a paradigm shift. Remembering a diagram shaped like an hourglass and showing the cross as the center of world history, one he had seen on a blackboard in his seminary days, Driver claims it is a "a dangerous picture."[10] Actually it is simply showing one biblical scholar's interpretation of the theology of Luke-Acts. For Luke, Jerusalem is the *omphalos*, the navel, of the universe. All Jewish history flows into the city; all Christian mission flows out from Jerusalem to Judea and Samaria "and to the ends of the earth" (Acts 1:8). In Driver's judgment, however, the scandal of believing that all salvation has come from one man, Jesus, is immoral as well as intellectually indefensible.

Dialogue between world religions is increasing. Gone (or almost gone) are the arrogance and condescension of nineteenth-century hymnody which relegated all non-Christians from Greenland's icy mountains to India's coral strands to the status of heathens waiting for rescue from darkness, but Christians have had to rethink the purpose and process of Christian mission in a pluralistic age. Some still cling to what Paul Clasper in his *Eastern Paths and the Christian Way* has called "the dungeon model": they believe that those who have not been freed by the good news of Jesus Christ are locked in a dark, cramped existence.[11] Clasper contrasts this dungeon model with the other extreme, what he calls "the round table model." There no one sits at the head of the table; instead, through careful listening to one another, everyone is enriched. Between these two extremes is a middle way, one which seeks to do justice both to the uniqueness and the universality of the Christian faith. Christ is "the crown" of every other path to God, even though there is much to be learned from the other traditions. Clasper sees rough consensus on this model today, while recognizing its dangers; to Hindus and Buddhists, for example, it may well seem to be just a slightly more sophisticated form of the old imperialism.

In his superb book on the Christian mission, *The Go-Between God*, Bishop John V. Taylor says that the Holy Spirit has been at work in all ages and all cultures, pointing to and bearing witness to the Logos. "Every religion has been a tradition of response to him," he writes, "however darkly it groped toward him, however anxiously it shied away from him." Just as the Christ fulfills Judaism, so he will fulfill Hinduism, Islam, Buddhism, and even the best of scientific humanism. Taylor summarizes succinctly: "Christ is not the property of us Christians."[12]

Questions about salvation at the end of the twentieth century clearly must include an awareness of and concern for our whole planet. We need to ask these questions, I think, in social terms rather than in the individualistic terms of nineteenth century pietism, when the question was often phrased, "What must I do to be saved?" Social salvation was really what the bishops at Nicea were thinking about when they stressed that it was *for us and for our salvation* that Jesus Christ came. Today, however, we are probably more likely to ask questions about salvation that arise out of the morning headlines—questions that have to do with AIDS and drugs and inner city crime, as well as the salvation of our planet from environmental destruction. What must we, as co-creators, do to help save our fragile earth?

Before we leave the question of salvation, I want to mention one more hymn with a very distinctive idea of the Atonement. It is a modern hymn and not firmly rooted in Scripture or tradition, although not alien to it, and it illustrates once more the importance of asking new questions about old doctrines, of letting fresh air into the halls of faith.

Back when Gerald Ford was President, the story goes, the executive board of the WCTU sent him a telegram urging him to ban a hymn in the new *Book of Worship for United States Forces*. The Chief of Chaplains of the Veterans' Administration actually ordered the offending hymn, "It Was on a Friday Morning," ripped from all copies of the new book belonging to the Veterans' Administration, many thousands of them, all within twenty-four hours.

The hymn may have been deeply offensive to the many people who found it blasphemous, especially when confronted with the line, "To hell with Jehovah," but it is not heretical. Instead, in the words of a *Christian Century* editorial, it is "a rather distinctive reinterpretation of the atonement"—one that raises the question of the guilt of God in Christ's death, and also of God's ultimate responsibility for sin and suffering in the world. The whole hymn is really an extended commentary on Acts 2:23, where Peter says Jesus was "handed over to you according to the definite plan and foreknowledge of God." Sidney Carter, author of the hymn, puts the words in the mouth of the thief hanging on the cross next to Jesus. The refrain is:

> It's God they ought to crucify
> Instead of you or me,
> I said to the carpenter
> A-hanging on the tree.[13]

Endnotes

1. The Hymnal 1982, 208

2. From "The Great Catechism" as excerpted in Robert L. Ferm, ed., *Readings in the History of Christian Thought* (New York: Holt, Rinehart and Winston, 1964), p. 202.

3. The Hymnal 1982, 162.

4. The Hymnal 1982, 167.

5. Cited by J. Ramsay McCallum, *Abelard's Christian Theology* (London: Basil Blackwell, 1948), p. 101.

6. Gordon Leff, *Medieval Thought: St. Augustine to Ockham* (New York: Penguin, 1958), p. 111.

7. Helen Wadell, *Peter Abelard* (New York: Viking Press, 1959), p. 257.

8. The Hymnal 1982, 164.

9. Virginia Fabella and Mercy Amba Oduyoye, eds., *With Passion and Compassion: Third World Women Doing Theology* (Maryknoll, NY: Orbis, 1989), Foreword.

10. Tom F. Driver, *Christ in a Changing World: Toward an Ethical Christology* (New York: Crossroad, 1981), pp. 57ff.

11. Paul Clasper, *Eastern Paths and the Christian Way* (New York: Orbis Books, 1982), pp. 101-115.

12. John V. Taylor, *The Go-Between God: The Holy Spirit and the Christian Mission* (London: Oxford University Press, 1972), p. 191.

13. As quoted in the editorial by Ronald Goetz, *The Christian Century* (October 6, 1976).

Chapter 6

Who is God the Spirit?

We believe in the Holy Spirit,
the Lord, the giver of life,
who proceeds from the Father and the Son.
With the Father and the Son
he is worshiped and glorified.
He has spoken through the Prophets.

"Come Holy Spirit—Renew the Whole Creation," the theme of the 1991 Assembly of the World Council of Churches held in Canberra, Australia in February of that year, marks the first time the theme of the Holy Spirit has been central in World Council meetings. It is also the first time the theme of an assembly has been phrased as a prayer. All the official participants were assigned to one of four sections, each representing one of the sub-themes of the meeting. They addressed God the Spirit as "Giver of Life," "Spirit of Truth," "Spirit of Unity," and simply "Holy Spirit." In this chapter we will ask about each of these aspects of "pneumatology," as the doctrine of the

Spirit is called. All of them are at least implicit in what the creed affirms about the Spirit.

First, it must be admitted that the church was slow to recognize the full personhood of the third *persona* of the Trinity, tending instead to be binitarian in practice. For the first few centuries of the church questions about the relationship between God and Jesus Christ occupied the attention of its leaders, while relatively little discussion of the being of God the Spirit took place. Only after the Council of Nicea did questions arise about what it meant to say, as Nicea did at the end of its creed, "and in the Holy Spirit."

Thinking about the Spirit has also been affected by the traditional language used by English speakers. The idea of a "Holy Ghost" causes people today to think of a Halloween spook rather than of God in action, although that was the way "Holy Spirit" was translated in the King James Version of the Bible, and English prayerbooks used the same phrase from 1549 until very recently. Children in particular find that ghostly designation confusing nowadays.

Further confusion arose from the major symbol that is used for God the Spirit, the symbol of a dove. In contrast to the personal metaphors of "Father" and "Son" that are used of the first two *personae* of the Trinity, the idea of a dove leads to people speaking of God the Spirit in neutral terms—as an "it." The God of the Bible is always a personal agent, however, and must be referred to in personal terms. Even though all four gospels say that at Jesus' baptism the Spirit descended upon him like a dove, the picture of a holy bird can cause misguided humor. When he was upset by the enthusiasm of the Anabaptists at the time of the Reformation, Martin Luther is reported to have said contemptuously, "They seem to have swallowed the Holy Spirit, feathers and all."

Section 1 of the World Council of Churches Assembly had as its full title, "Giver of Life—Sustain Your Creation." Something has already been said in Chapter 3 about God the Spirit's role in creation, both the creation of the cosmos and the creation of human life. In the Adam narrative God *breathes* into the nostrils of the inert earthling the "breath of life," and the creature becomes "a living being." The Hebrew word for "spirit," as well as for "breath" and for "wind," is *ruach*. The Greek word *pneuma* has the same three meanings. Which of the three words is used in the English depends entirely on the context and the judgment of the translators. Where the Revised Standard Version translates Genesis 1:2 as "the Spirit of God" moving over the face of the waters, for example, the Jewish Publication Society's Torah reads "a wind from God."

In Canberra the delegates were intensely aware of the dangers of human damage to the created order, which could be fatal to this planet. The Spirit as "Giver of Life" is defiantly opposed by human beings. In the Bible study on the topic for this group, one of the assigned passages was Romans 8:1-27, in which Paul speaks of a "new creation." It is a difficult text to understand. Paul says,

> For the creation was subjected to futility, not of its own will but by the will of the one who subjected it,

in hope that the creation itself will be set free from its bondage to decay and will obtain the freedom of the glory of the children of God. We know that the whole creation has been groaning in labor pains until now; and not only the creation, but we ourselves, who have the first fruits of the Spirit, groan inwardly. (vv. 20-23)

Commentators disagree on what Paul had in mind in this passage. One scholar thinks he may be alluding to current astrological beliefs, according to which all of creation lying below the planetary spheres was enslaved to the celestial powers above it; another thinks that Paul was referring to the myth in Genesis 3 wherein the ground is cursed because of Adam's disobedience, making it difficult to wrest a living from the earth. Whatever Paul was talking about in this passage, it very clearly links the future of creation to the idea of hope, and the hope of glory at that.

In the official report of this section at the conclusion of the assembly, however, the note of hope is hard to find. Instead, the enormous seriousness of our ecological crises dominates. The report gives a new interpretation to Paul's idea in Romans 8: while "the Spirit has never abandoned the creation or ceased from sustaining it," the report says, "the earth on which we live is in peril. Creation protests its treatment by human beings. It groans and travails in all its parts." The report concludes gloomily, "The only future foreshadowed by the present crisis is massive suffering, both human and other than human."[1]

God the Spirit is also associated with truth and unity in the New Testament, as well as with the creation of life. Three times in his farewell discourse in the Fourth Gospel Jesus speaks of God the Spirit as the Spirit of Truth (Jn. 14:17; 15:16; 16:13). Jesus also promised his disciples, "You will know the truth and the truth will make you free" (Jn. 8:32). The Spirit is called the *paraclete*, a word that is difficult to translate and a concept which New Testament scholar Raymond E. Brown calls "a many-splendored thing." The King James Version of the Bible has added to the confusion by translating *paraclete* as "comforter." Although at that time the Latin root meaning "with strength" was clear to people, all too often modern people have thought of the Spirit as the equivalent of a warm, cozy quilt to cuddle under. Two contemporary versions of the Bible, the RSV and the NRSV, use "counselor" and "advocate."

Both counselors and advocates are familiar to us as people who speak up or speak out for someone else. God the Spirit, the Nicene Creed tells us, spoke through the prophets. The prophets of the Bible were the prime social critics of their day; they were the ones who shook up the religious establishment, too. They rocked the boat. The Spirit is "Lord of the unexpected"—the one who, in John V. Taylor's fine phrase, "appears not to have read the rubrics."[2]

Undoubtedly this quality of unpredictability is one of the reasons that the church has never felt quite at ease with God the Spirit. Throughout the history of the church, periodic outbursts of religious enthusiasm have meant that "enthusiasm" has become a pejorative term, even though its root means simply *en theos*, in-Godded.

One such early movement of religious fervor is known as Montanism. It is the prototype of almost everything modern Pentecostalism represents. A Christian named Montanus began to prophesy in the province of Phrygia about the year 172. He claimed that he himself was the promised Paraclete, the Spirit of Truth, and that he was bringing a new revelation. He was joined by two women, Priscilla and Maximilla by name, who insisted that God also spoke through them—"the diffusion of the prophetic spirit even among women," as one historian has put it. The Montanists were against hierarchy, which is one of the reasons why the church distrusted them and perhaps also why the sect spread so rapidly. Whole cities in Syria went over to "the reformers," as they were called. Within five years Montanism had reached Rome and Lyons; its most famous convert was the "father of Latin theology," Tertullian. The historian Eusebius calls the movement both heretical and schismatic. One is reminded of that line in the hymnbook, "by schisms rent asunder, by heresies distressed."

An equally notable "heretic" in the eyes of the papacy was one Joachim of Fiore, founder and abbot of a new branch of the Cistercians in the twelfth century. Joachim divided the history of the world into three overlapping ages, those of Father and Son and Holy Spirit. The Age of the Father began with Adam and ended with Christ; the Age of the Son began with Christ and would end, Joachim predicted, in 1260 when the Age of the Spirit would begin. He chose that date by a complex process of biblical dating, calculating forty-two generations for each of the ages, averaging thirty years apiece.

Since Joachim died at the beginning of the thirteenth century, he did not live to see the Age of the Spirit. Before that year came, he was condemned posthumously by the Fourth Lateran Council—not for his theory of history but for his doctrine of the Trinity, set forth in a treatise now lost. But his vision of a new age set Europeans dreaming, unleashing a revolutionary imagination. The idea of a coming Age of the Spirit led to criticism of the existing voices of authority, both religious and social. The One who speaks through the prophets always unsettles the establishment. Dante placed Joachim in Paradise, along with the other great mystics.

The idea of unity has long been associated with God the Spirit. Indeed, theologian John Macquarrie calls the Spirit simply Unitive Being in his *Principles of Christian Theology*. The Father, in Macquarrie's terminology, is Primordial Being, while the Son, or Word, is Expressive Being. As Unitive Being, the Holy Spirit is, as it were, the mutual love exchanged within the Godhead. God is love apart from God's outgoing love for all creation. Eastern orthodoxy has long spoken of *perichoresis* to refer to the interpenetration of the *personae* in the Triune Being, almost a divine dance of love.

As Unitive Being, God the Spirit, according to the creedal statement we have before us, "proceeds from the Father and the Son." The phrase "and the Son" is that infamous *filioque* we discussed briefly in Chapter 2. Not only is love exchanged within the Godhead through the Spirit, but the Spirit is also shared with human beings. How are we recipients of God's Spirit? Is the Spirit a gift from God the Father, or from Jesus Christ, or both?

John's gospel appears to answer that question in two ways. John 15:26 speaks of "the Spirit of truth who comes from the Father." (In earlier translations, the word "proceeds" was used instead of "comes from," hence the idea of a procession). At the end of the gospel, however, the Risen Lord breathes on the disciples and says to them, "Receive the Holy Spirit" (20:22). Breath is itself, of course, a Spirit word, reminding one of the Creator God who breathed into Adam's nostrils to give life. The first text appears to support what is known as the "single procession"; the second, the "double procession." The first is the view of the Eastern Orthodox, the second of the western church. Is this just a quibble over words or is something important at stake?

John Macquarrie thinks the question is a real and substantive issue. The western view has the merit, he says, of linking the Spirit closely to the Son, thus giving content to an otherwise rather vague concept of the Holy Spirit. It also ties the Spirit closely to the Logos— emotion and intellect knit together, as it were. On the other hand, Macquarrie thinks, the eastern emphasis avoids the dangers of subordinating the Spirit to the Son, as they think westerners tend to do.[3] Sometimes the Spirit is made to sound almost like a junior partner in the Godhead.

A frequent suggestion, and one that has wide appeal to many contemporary theologians, is a compromise between the two views. Why not say that the Spirit proceeds from the Father *through* the Son? This seems to do justice to the biblical witness, and it also might help toward ecumenical reconciliation on the issue.

The Spirit is not confined to the Christian church. Hans Küng made the same point nicely when he wrote, "The Spirit of God, if domiciled in the Church, is not domesticated in it. He is and remains the free Spirit of the Lord...not only of Christians, but of the whole world."[4]

Another New Testament account of the gift of the Spirit sounds to me, however, as if the Spirit's chief sphere of operation is within the church. This is the familiar story of Pentecost, which Luke tells early in the Acts of the Apostles. The disciples are all together in one place. They suddenly hear the sound of a rushing mighty wind. Then they see tongues of fire resting on each of them: "All of them were filled with the Holy Spirit and began to speak in other languages, as the Spirit gave them ability" (Acts 2:4).

Consider wind and fire first. Wind is experienced as something both benign and frightening. It can be a cool evening breeze on a hot day, perhaps, or a fresh wind filling the sails on your boat. On the other hand, it is the destructive power of a tornado or the fierce fury of a hurricane.

Fire is similarly ambiguous. What is more conducive to cozy feelings than a fire crackling in your fireplace on a cold night, or the coals of a campfire at last just right for toasting marshmallows? But fire is also capable of running out of control. If you've ever been in even a small forest fire, much less a burning house, you know how terrifying it can be. Remember those images of blazing oil wells, that inferno Iraq left behind in Kuwait after the Gulf War?

In the two major symbols for Pentecost we meet again the duality that is the hallmark of holiness, that same duality of awe and attractiveness we met in considering "the Father, the *Pantocrator*" in Chapter 2. Somehow it seems entirely appropriate that the Holy Spirit of God comes with rushing wind and tongues of fire, symbols every bit as full of fascinating invitation and full of the power of dynamite.

The Pentecost story as it stands is unclear about what kind of speaking in other languages is described. On one level the story is intentionally a reversal of the Tower of Babel myth in Genesis: in the Genesis tale, the Lord confused human language. Whereas at first "the whole earth had one language and the same words" (11:1), the Lord deliberately made people unable to understand one another's language in order to curb human hubris. On this level, the Acts account undoes that disaster: "How is it that we hear, each of us, in our own native language?" The amazed, devout Jews were gathered in Jerusalem "from every nation under heaven."

At the same time, the narrative tells us that the disciples were accused of being drunk—and early in the morning, at that. This sounds much more like the "speaking in tongues," known as *glossolalia*, which Paul encountered in the church at Corinth. Indeed Paul

76

claims to speak in tongues himself: "I thank God that I speak in tongues more than all of you; nevertheless, in church I would rather speak five words with my mind, in order to instruct others also, than ten thousand words in a tongue" (1 Cor. 14:18-19).

Paul utters this judgment in the midst of his well-known discussion of "gifts of the Spirit" in chapters 12-14 of his first letter to the Corinthians, the one in which the beloved hymn on love occurs. (The list of gifts of the Spirit in this section ranges all the way from the working of miracles to administration, and it is good to know that God the Spirit is as concerned about good administration as about miracle workers.) The idea of spiritual gifts has, alas, caused almost as much divisiveness in the church as it has created unity. In particular that has been the case in reaction to the so-called Neo-Pentecostals, an outbreak of the unexpected in the churches that began in the sixties. The phenomenon was startling to many—Roman Catholic undergraduates at Yale University suddenly speaking in tongues? Episcopalians in Van Nuys, California, prophesying? Unthinkable—but it happened, and it is still happening in the various renewal movements in the churches.

In July of 1991, charismatic Christians from over one hundred nations came together in Brighton, England; over three thousand people from eleven denominations.[5] It was an International Consultation on World Evangelization. These Christians all spoke of "baptism in the Holy Spirit," a powerful personal experience of the Spirit's presence frequently manifested in the spontaneous outburst of the prayer-language called "speak-

ing in tongues." A former student of mine, a high-rank-
ing naval officer, once told me of having such an experience while riding in a taxi, in full dress uniform, headed
for the Pentagon. The Spirit is not bound by rules of
decorum.

Reports from the Brighton conference indicate that
in this week-long meeting leaders from the charismatic
movement around the world seemed more open to col-
laboration with other Christians and were "moderating
their elitist claims"—which is one of the charges once-
born Christians make against the twice-born. All too
often the Christian without experience of "baptism in
the Spirit" is made to feel second-class.

A striking example of this was cited in one of the
questions for discussion following the World Council of
Churches' Bible study on "The Spirit of Unity." The
question centered on the experience of a Scandinavian
Christian in the Holy Land who had signed up for a
course in glossolalia, in spite of the fact that tongues are
said to be a special gift of the Spirit and not a learned
technique. This person tried for five days but did not
succeed in speaking in tongues. As a consequence the
group cut its ties with him because they thought he
lacked "a clear sign of true faith."[6]

Finally, in this chapter, we should ask about the sen-
tence of the creed which says of the Spirit, "With the
Father and the Son he is worshiped and glorified." Why
is it there? What does it add to our understanding of
the Spirit?

At the time of the Council of Constantinople, the
council that adopted the expanded statement on the

Holy Spirit we find now in this third paragraph, a question troubling the church was whether God the Spirit was coequal to God the Father and the Son. What was the status of the Holy Spirit? A group of Christians called Pneumatomachians or Macedonians taught that the Holy Spirit was a creature, one of the ministering angels, a position similar to that of Arius in connection with the Logos doctrine.

The emperor Theodosius called the Second Ecumenical Council in 381 in order to bring peace to the church. Its chief purpose was to clarify the question, is the Holy Spirit fully and completely God? The council adopted the phrase we have before us, "With the Father and the Son," to settle the matter. God the Spirit was declared coequal and coeternal with the Father and Son, yet the bishops hesitated to reuse the term *homoousious*, one in Being, used of the Son by Nicea. If God the Spirit is worshiped and glorified together with Father and Son, however, the effect is the same. The Pneumatomachians are said to have packed their bags and left Constantinople before the decision was taken, but they were anathematized by the council anyway. Basil, the great Cappadocian theologian, was the chief spokesman against their position.

Today our questions about the Holy Spirit are different from those of the fourth century. Is it likely, perhaps, that nowadays we would ask more about how the Spirit makes a difference in our own lives? In one way or another, I suspect we might wonder about what Paul means when he tells us we are "called to be saints" (1 Cor. 1:2). The question raises the topic of sanctification, which is a process of gradual transformation through which God's Spirit works to help the human spirit grow closer to God. Quite simply, it is growth in the Christian life, in Christian love. It has nothing to do with feeling holy, and even less with feeling holier-than-thou. Sanctimoniousness is the very antithesis of sanctification.

Paul was definitely in favor of sanctification, in spite of his reputation at the time of the Reformation of being interested only in justification by faith, that is, being accounted righteous rather than becoming righteous. Even in the chapters of Romans where he emphasizes justification most strongly, Paul exhorts Christians to yield their "members as slaves to righteousness for sanctification" (Rom. 6:19). Shortly thereafter he says, "But now that you have been freed from sin and enslaved to God, the advantage you get is sanctification. The end is eternal life" (6:22).

The wisdom of the council in relating the idea of worship to God the Spirit becomes very clear when we think about sanctification. Worship is the activity in which we open our spirits to God's Spirit. For several generations many Christians (perhaps especially Anglicans) were uncomfortable talking about their spiritual lives. Now there is a new interest in spirituality; the word has become almost overworked, in fact. Is there a danger that in talking so much about spirituality we may forget that we are embodied creatures, and not purely spiritual? Is there enough emphasis today on community spirit, not just on the individual? In short, what is God the Spirit doing today, both in the church and in the rest of the world? Perhaps that is the key question we need to ask again and again.

Endnotes

1. Michael Kinnamon, ed., *Signs of the Spirit*, Official Report of the Seventh Assembly, World Council of Churches (Geneva: WCC Publications, 1991), p. 55.

2. Taylor, *The Go-Between God*, p. 120.

3. John Macquarrie, *Principles of Christian Theology*, 2d edition (Charles Scribner & Sons, 1977), p. 331.

4. Hans Küng, *The Church* (New York: Sheed and Ward, 1967), p. 176.

5. See "Charismatics at Brighton," *Ecumenical Trends* 21 (March 1992), for the participants' reports.

6. *"Come Holy Spirit—Renew the Whole Creation": Six Bible Studies* (Geneva: WCC Publications, 1989), p. 80.

Chapter 7

What is the Church?

*We believe in one holy catholic
and apostolic church.*

"I t's just that the church doesn't do anything for them," a *New York Times* story announced recently in trying to explain why mainline Protestant churches have lost millions of members in the past quarter of a century. Reporting the results of a major new study of the Presbyterian Church just completed under the auspices of the Lilly Foundation, the account said, "Only twenty-nine percent of the people interviewed who were confirmed in the church remain active." Forty-eight percent of those surveyed were classified as unchurched. "Many don't see the church as essential to their faith," the researchers concluded. They think that they "can be a good Christian without doing it in the context of the church."[1]

Why does the Christian creed claim that the church is an essential article of the faith? Four assertions about the church pop out at anyone reading or reciting the Nicene Creed, and each of them appears manifestly contrary to what you know to be true as you look about at the churches you know best. How can we claim that the church is "one" when over two hundred different denominations are listed in the almanac? How can we say that the church is "holy" when most of its members are no better than you and me? Or "catholic"? Look at the bitter fighting between Protestant and Catholic in northern Ireland, for example; what is that all about if the whole church is catholic? As for "apostolic," do you mean loyal to the teaching of the apostles, or to some claim of authority, or what?

That the church is "one, holy, catholic, and apostolic" has long been designated the four "marks" or "notes" of the Christian church, but each of these adjectives raises troubling questions about their empirical reality. We will look at each of them in turn in this chapter and try at least to clear away some of the obstacles that stand in the way of anyone's saying with integrity "we believe" in a church so described.

Unity among Christians has always been a problem in the church. As early as the year 55, the church in the Greek city of Corinth was beset with divisions, divisions which the apostle Paul tackled directly in his first letter to that community. Some of "Chloe's people" brought Paul a report about the quarrels among them. It would be nice to know to which of the "parties" in the Corinthian church these rumor-bearers belonged. Paul's answer was intended to be read aloud when the church next assembled for worship. Why were they saying that they belonged to Apollos or to Cephas or to Paul himself? He asks a rhetorical question of the kind he often used: "Has Christ been divided?" Stop boasting about your favorite leader, he tells them, before proceeding to deal with the question of sexual immorality in the church. Stop boasting; remember that "you belong to Christ, and Christ belongs to God" (1 Cor. 3:23).

The church of God, as Paul calls it in the opening salutation of this letter, appears always to have had centrifugal as well as centripetal forces at work within it. Very seldom has it been possible to say, as Luke does of the believers shortly after Pentecost, that "all who believed were together and had all things in common" (Acts 2:44). They cannot all have been together physically in one place, since there were more than three thousand of them, according to Acts; rather, "the whole group of those who believed were of one heart and soul" (Acts 4:32). Two chapters later, however, Acts reports that when the disciples increased in number and ethnic diversity, the Hellenists complained against the Hebrews because they thought they were not getting their fair share of community food (6:1). That was shortly before what has been called the first ecumenical conference met at Jerusalem to settle differences between these two groups.

The Council of Jerusalem reached a decision that is of immense significance for our understanding of the church's unity. It was decided that no one was required to be circumcised and to keep the law of Moses in order to be a Christian. In other words, Jew and Gentile alike could be part of the one church. Unity did not and does not mean uniformity. As the poet Phyllis McGinley put it many years ago in praising diversity, "After all, even God is said to be three persons."

The modern ecumenical movement grew out of ecumenical conferences on two different subjects that began in 1910 and met about every ten years until they merged to form what is now the World Council of Churches. The archbishop of Canterbury, William Temple, was a leader in causing the merger of the Faith and Order Conference with that on Life and Work. The Second World War made it necessary to postpone the first world assembly, however, and it finally occurred in Amsterdam in 1948. The most recent one, of which we talked in the last chapter, was the seventh such world meeting.

A conciliar model of unity falls far short of what many Christians think one church should look like, however. They seek visible unity, the kind of unity they think the author of Ephesians meant in saying, "There is one body and one Spirit, just as you were called to the one hope of your calling, one Lord, one faith, one baptism, one God and Father of all, who is above all and through all and in all" (4:4-6). Two kinds of efforts are being made to this end—multilateral and bilateral dialogues.

In the United States, one prominent example of the first type called itself the Consultation on Church Unity and quickly acquired the unfortunate acronym COCU as a result. Members of COCU were representatives from some twelve or thirteen participating denominations, meeting in plenary sessions year by year, trying to hammer out a statement of an agreed faith.

After some twenty years of work, the plenary, which by 1984 had only nine denominational delegations, was able to adopt a consensus called, significantly, "In Quest of a Church of Christ Uniting." The change of emphasis makes clear that uniting is a process. The consensus speaks of the nature of unity not as a merger but as a "diversity-in-communion." It argues strongly that visible unity is essential "that the world may believe." A mission thrust mandates it. Anyone can see that in India, for example, where Christians are less than two percent of the population, small and petty differences between, say, Anglicans and Presbyterians are absurdly irrelevant in proclaiming the gospel.

The consensus report lists seven characteristics of a Church Uniting that make it truly catholic, truly evangelical, and truly reformed. They include the centrality of celebrating God's grace, an ongoing mission of salvation for the whole world, an apostolic and priestly ministry for every church member, structures that mirror the diversity of its membership, appreciation for the several traditions of participating churches, strengthening of previous ecumenical relations, and maximum openness for continuing renewal and reformation.[2]

It is of particular interest to our creedal agenda that the consensus acknowledges both the Apostles' and the Nicene creeds as "unique ecumenical witnesses" which the Church Uniting will use in worship as "acts of praise and allegiance to the Triune God." This consensus statement was recommended to the nine member denominations for study and reception.

More typical of ecumenical efforts in recent years has been the bilateral dialogue between two denominations. These go on simultaneously. The Anglican Communion, for example, is currently engaged in separate international dialogues with Lutheran, Roman Catholic, Orthodox, and Reformed churches. Each of the dialogue partners is also talking with an equal number of other people. Since each dialogue is made up of different individuals, a clear danger exists that an agreed statement of one bilateral conversation will differ widely from an agreed statement emerging from another. The whole procedure is both cumbersome and expensive.

In more recent thinking and practice, a kind of grassroots ecumenism exists that is showing impatience with the whole search for institutional unity. This means that on the local level many Christians see all baptized persons as members of Christ's church and feel no barriers to full communion with them. Far more urgent are newer issues such as racism and sexism and congregational exclusivism. It is widely recognized that such issues are far more divisive than traditional issues such as your idea of the authority of Scripture or my views on justification by faith. Why, for example, do congregations of all one race continue to exist? Furthermore, the most pervasive instance of sexism in the churches is perhaps the continued use of older translations of the Bible that do not use inclusive language. In 1895 Elizabeth Cady Stanton wrote, "From the inauguration of the movement for woman's emancipation the Bible has been used to hold her in the 'divinely ordained sphere,' prescribed in the Old and New Testaments."[3] Not until the 1990s was it possible for a woman to hear in readings in church that Paul, for example, really wrote to "brothers and sisters," or that she was not intended to become a "son of God."

It is also recognized by some that "the Coming Great Church," as it has been called, will be far, far more diverse than the churches of the western world have ever been. Such phenomena as Christian base communities in Latin America, or the newer indigenous African Christian groups, offer a richly textured future of the church far beyond the current ecclesial variety.

Although the second mark of the church is "holy," I want to discuss "catholic" first. In talking of unity, the search for visible unity, the ecumenical movement was the focus. "Ecumenical" comes from a Greek word meaning "the whole inhabited earth," whereas "catholic" comes from a Greek word meaning "universal." First used, as far as we know, by a Syrian bishop, Ignatius of Antioch, in one of his letters written while en route to martyrdom in Rome about the year 107, it came in time to mean what all Christians have believed at all times, everywhere—that is, the orthodox faith. It does not mean acknowledging the supremacy of the Pope. Catholic Christians who are not Roman Catholics should help their Roman Catholic friends to use the adjective Roman if they mean what the Reformers called papists. John Calvin, in fact, wanted to restore "the face of the ancient Catholic Church."

A test of catholicity today might well be agreement with the Chicago-Lambeth Quadrilateral setting forth the four criteria for a uniting church—the Holy Scriptures of the Old and New Testaments as containing all things necessary to salvation, the two historic creeds as a sufficient summary of the Christian faith, the two sacraments of baptism and eucharist ordained by Christ as essential, and the historic episcopate "locally adapted in the methods of its administration to the varying needs of the nations."

Just as "one" and "catholic" are not sharply distinguished in thought about the church, so too is there overlap between catholic and "apostolic." The word "apostle" comes from the Greek word meaning "one who is sent forth." According to the agreed statement of the Anglican-Orthodox dialogue accepted at Dublin in 1984, the church's apostolicity is manifested through the succession of bishops and this succession is a sign of the unbroken continuity of apostolic tradition and life. More fully, the statement asserts that apostolic tradition is maintained in the preaching and teaching of the church, in its apostolic mission to the world, as well as the succession of bishops.

A far more ecumenical statement puts it even more bluntly: the episcopal succession is "a sign, though not a guarantee," of the continuity and unity of the church.[4] No pipeline theory of the episcopate is endorsed, one that would lead you to think that the pedigree of a bishop could be traced back through who laid hands on whom—from the bishop of Buffalo today, say, back to the apostle Peter. Such a tactile succession simply cannot be defended historically.

An outward and forward thrust of apostolicity is also equally essential along with the backward look. People are still being sent out in mission to bring other people to Jesus Christ. A case can be made, indeed, that one of the first apostles was the Samaritan woman in John's gospel. Jesus sent her home to bring people to him: "She said to the people, 'Come and see a man who told me everything I have ever done! He cannot be the Messiah, can he?' They left the city and were on their way to him" (Jn. 4:28-30).

"Holiness" is the fourth mark of the church. This is claimed to be an appropriate adjective because the members are in Christ, the Head, who is holy. That is easy enough to say, but the holiness is certainly obscured, if not obliterated, by the behavior of its members. The old chestnut that the church is not a club for saints but a hospital for sinners needs to be balanced by Paul's address to the bickering Corinthian Christians. They are, he says, "called to be saints." No halo is required, but the call to walk in love must be heeded—and heard over and over again. That is the call to sanctification through the power of the Holy Spirit.

Holiness is by no means limited to the church. The holy God charges the world with God's grandeur and God's holiness. In a powerful little book called *Holy the Firm*, Annie Dillard sees as clearly as did Gerard Manley Hopkins that "holiness holds forth in time." She is also intensely aware of all the seeming evil in the world. Dillard asks, with the psalmist, "Who shall ascend unto the hill of the Lord? or who shall stand in His holy place?" and she answers, "There is no one but us." Dillard says she knows only enough of God to want to worship God. Since she lives on an island in Puget Sound where there is only one church, she worships at this white frame church set among the fir trees. Only about twenty other people attend, all of them over sixty years old. Dillard admits it sometimes makes her feel as if she were on an archaeological tour of Soviet Russia, yet she volunteers to bring wine for communion. "Are there holy grapes," she asks, "is there holy ground, is anything here holy?" "No," she answers herself, "there are no holy grapes, there is no holy ground, nor is there anyone but us."[5]

Nowhere else in contemporary literature have I met anyone as sensitive to the absurdity of calling the church holy, or as aware of the necessity of doing so. Because, of course, the church is *us*, all baptized Christians.

Our inherited vocabulary about the nature of the Christian church makes some additional distinctions that we need to look at before we explore what questions today's Christians are asking. From the Reformation we have two pairs of terms, the church "militant and triumphant" and the church "visible and invisible." What did they mean then, and are they useful today?

The first distinction, that between the church militant and triumphant, was meant to discourage prayer for the dead. By calling the Christians already in heaven "the church triumphant" and divorcing that group from Christians still fighting the good fight on earth, who were "the church militant," such prayer could be effectively discouraged.

One of the complaints the Reformers made about the Church of Rome, of course, concerned what they called

Romish superstitions. The Thirty-Nine Articles of Religion in the Church of England, for example, said in the kind of blunt language you would not hear in ecumenical dialogue today, "The Romish Doctrine concerning Purgatory, Pardons, Worshipping and Adoration, as well of Images as of Relics, and also Invocation of Saints, is a fond thing, vainly invented, and grounded upon no warranty of Scripture, but rather repugnant to the Word of God."

So opposed were the Reformers to the invocation of saints that they banned any prayer whatsoever for the dead, at least some of whom were presumably in heaven and hence members of "the church triumphant." To make sure that no one thought the dead were being prayed *for*, much less *to*, what in 1549 was called the "Prayer for the Whole State of Christ's Church" in the 1552 Book of Common Prayer began with the bidding, "Let us pray for the whole state of Christ's Church *militant here on earth*." But then, the Litany in that same edition prayed for deliverance from "the tyranny of the Bishop of Rome and all his detestable enormities."

These rabid anti-Roman sentiments of mid-century Anglicans came, by 1600, to be moderated considerably. The judicious Richard Hooker was equally unhappy that both Rome and Geneva would admit no error. As for the church, however, Hooker defined it in such a way that he disposed of the militant-triumphant dichotomy entirely. He called it a "supernatural society," meaning a single community that includes God, angels, and men and women, living and dead.

The distinction between visible and invisible churches was also seized upon by the Reformers to distinguish themselves from the visible institution of the medieval church of the Pope. John Calvin, for example, held that the Scriptures speak of the church in two ways—the church as it really is before God (i.e., all the elect), and as the whole body of baptized Christians, which includes all the hypocrites. He thought that both must be called the church, nevertheless, and we must cultivate communion with the visible church.

The distinction between visible and invisible churches is very much with us still, although in slightly modified form. That form was evident in the *Times* article quoted at the beginning of this chapter. It is customary for many people to scorn what they call "the institutional church," as if there were some other kind. This is equivalent to the visible church of the other terminology. An ideal church or a happy *koinonia*, a Christian fellowship without the burden of budgets and buildings and bank accounts, is the equivalent of an invisible church, I suppose. People rarely say exactly what they mean when they dismiss the institutional church, but in my judgment there is always an institutional dimension of the Christian church, and has been since Pentecost.

In *Of the Laws of Ecclesiastical Polity*, Richard Hooker again demolishes the distinction between "visible and invisible." Hooker says that the church has the same basis as any other society or association. He is writing, of course, about political structures, the governing laws of the church. "By the Church," he says, "we understand no other than only the visible Church."[6] Hooker uses the analogy of the whole body of the ocean being one, yet divided into seas with different names. So it is with the catholic church, which is divided into a number of distinct societies, each called a church.

Throughout this book we are in the process of celebrating Christian doubt and raising questions. The Nicene Creed is, as it were, a punching bag—something to push against, at least, if not to fight. If you were asked today to choose four adjectives to describe your concept of the church, without necessarily abandoning the four we have inherited, what would you choose?

In the New Testament, as Paul Minear has shown superbly well, the word *ecclesia* or church means an assembly, a community of believers, a community gathered by God through Jesus Christ, and the eschatological people of God—those gathered from among the nations to participate in the new age that the Messiah inaugurates. In addition to these four different uses of the word "church," however, Minear has also identified ten cognate ways of expressing the idea of the church in the New Testament. It is the saints and the sanctified. It is all believers, all the faithful. In fifty passages in some eighteen New Testament writings, it is also slaves and servants. Although "people of God" is a major way of expressing the church idea, it is also possible in the New Testament to speak of the church as a family, or as a kingdom, or a new exodus, or as one body in Christ.[7]

Do any of these images work today? Which ones? Or do we need new images? I, for example, find it difficult to think of myself as part of a flock, one of the sheep in the fold. Do you? As we consider new images, we might do well to keep in mind something that Walter Brueggemann said recently. He voiced a serious concern in an article called "Rethinking Church Models Through Scripture" that we live in a time when the church's alliance with the dominant culture is being broken.[8] He wonders whether, in this situation, the church might be wise to reconsider the "wilderness-exile" models, models he associates with a time in post-exilic Judaism when the community of faith exercised little influence over public policy, when it had to develop "strategies and mechanisms for survival." If the church has again become a community at the margin, he suggests, it must think of itself as a community of exiles.

We may find it uncongenial, but there is no biblical evidence that the God of the Bible cringes at the prospect of the church community being one of wilderness and exile. How could we accomplish such a change in our self-image if we wanted to? Does the idea of the church as an exodus community conflict in any way with the creedal emphasis on a church that is one, holy, catholic, and apostolic?

Endnotes

1. *New York Times* (Sunday, June 7, 1992), p. 28.

2. Gerald F. Moede, ed., *The COCU Consensus: In Quest of a Church of Christ Uniting*, (Consultation on Church Union, 1985), pp. 12-14.

3. Elizabeth Cady Stanton, *The Woman's Bible* (Seattle: Coalition Task Force on Women and Religion, 1974; reprint ed.), p. 7.

4. *Baptism, Eucharist, and Ministry*, Faith and Order Paper No. 111 (Geneva: World Council of Churches, 1982), p. 29.

5. Annie Dillard, *Holy the Firm* (San Francisco: Harper & Row, 1988), pp. 56, 63.

6. Richard Hooker, *Of the Laws of Ecclesiastical Polity*, III. 1. 14.

7. Paul Minear, "Church, Idea of," *The Interpreter's Dictionary of the Bible*, Vol. 1. See also his *Images of the Church in the New Testament* (Philadelphia: Westminster Press, 1960).

8. Walter Brueggemann, "Rethinking Church Models Through Scripture," *Theology Today*, 48 (July 1991), pp. 128-138.

Chapter 8

What is Baptism?

*We acknowledge one baptism
for the forgiveness of sins.*

T
he title of one of my favorite twentieth-century paintings is "The Virgin Spanking Jesus as a Child Before Three Witnesses." Painted by Max Ernst in 1926, it now hangs in a museum in Cologne. The little boy lies naked across his mother's lap. Her hand is raised high, ready to descend on the small bottom with a resounding thwack, while three witnesses are peering through a small window at the back of the room. A delicious detail is the halo on the floor, slipped and fallen from the curly head.

The painting raises directly or indirectly at least four questions we are faced with in this chapter. What is sin? What does baptism have to do with the forgiveness of sin? What is forgiveness? And, if Jesus was sinless, as the tradition insists, why did he go to be baptized for the forgiveness of sins?

Orthodox Christianity has taught that Jesus was "sinless." In fact the Chalcedonian Definition, of which we spoke earlier, states that Jesus was like us in every re-spect except for sin. Yet he himself sought out his cousin John, who was administering baptisms in the Jordan "for the forgiveness of sins." Why?

If Jesus really were fully human he must have been a participant in corporate sin, the kind of systemic sin we will discuss shortly. He lived in an occupied country. He was aware of Roman oppression. He was part of a cul-ture that knew as much about governmental corruption as our own, as well as about hunger and poverty and disease. In his public ministry, Jesus worked against all of these sins of his culture, but he hadn't been unaf-fected by them as he was growing up and trying to fig-ure out what he was meant to do with his life. He may indeed have increased in wisdom and stature and in di-vine and human favor, but not automatically, without struggle. When Jesus disappeared for three days when he was twelve, we are supposed to marvel at his adoles-cent precociousness in discussing theology in the Tem-ple, but it is clear that Joseph and Mary were upset. What parents wouldn't be? His reported surprise at their anxiety is, to say the least, insensitive.

As you can tell, I do not think the idea of a sinless Je-sus is consistent either with the New Testament or with the assertion of his full humanity. Whatever Max Ernst thought Jesus did to deserve a spanking, I am grateful to him. It is cheering to think that Jesus' halo slipped from time to time.

In today's world, sin is no more popular a word than is salvation. It is so unpopular, in fact, that it has almost disappeared from the contemporary vocabulary, a fact which led a noted psychiatrist, Karl Menninger, to write a book twenty years ago with the title *Whatever Became of Sin?* Menninger says that the word sin was once "a strong word, an ominous and serious one"; nowadays something can be evil, disgraceful, corrupt, prejudicial, harmful, but it is not "sinful."[1] The idea of sin has become synonymous with crime or some psychological symptom, or it is seen as a matter of collective irresponsibility. Menninger remembers that in his youth the great sin was masturbation.

A contemporary discussion of sin requires at least three distinctions. First there is sin with a capital "S," meaning sinfulness, a state or condition. Second come sinful acts, which are sins in the plural, "lower-case" sins. And third, and perhaps most intransigent, is what I call systemic sin, sinful institutions. As C. S. Lewis put it in one of his science-fiction novels, we live in a "bent world."

On Ash Wednesday, the beginning of Lent, the collect for the day speaks of "lamenting our sins and acknowledging our wretchedness." This statement always seemed to me to be excessively extravagant, on a level with "the burden of them is intolerable," until I discovered belatedly that "wretched" is an old English term for exile. Thus it refers to our alienation, our separation from God. We are in a state of a broken relationship.

What broke this relationship? The myth of Eve and Adam suggests it was disobedience to God's command, a misuse of our freedom. Charged with the prohibition against eating the fruit of just one tree in the garden, the primordial couple couldn't resist. The narrator, the

99

Yahwist, says that when "the woman saw that the tree was good for food, and that it was a delight to the eyes, and that the tree was to be desired to make one wise, she took of its fruit and ate" (Gen. 3:6). I like the three reasons given, especially the appeal to aesthetic sensibility.

For centuries the woman was blamed for the Fall, as it is called. The New Testament itself says it was all Eve's fault: "Adam was not deceived, but the woman was deceived and became a transgressor" (1 Tim. 2:14). Tertullian called women "the gateway of evil." Only more recently has the philosopher Paul Ricoeur pointed out in *The Symbolism of Evil* that the story as we have it distributes the fault pretty evenly among the woman, the man, and the serpent.

Sin in the sense of a state or condition has been called, misleadingly, "original sin," the state or condition of everyone. One doesn't have to think of an inherited stain on the psyche, which has been passed on genetically; the condition of sin is a broken relationship with God and, as a consequence, alienation from each other and from ourselves. As one contemporary theologian put it powerfully, "Sin is when life freezes."

"Lower-case" sins, in the plural, are a different matter. They are acts, acts stemming from a built-in bias on our own behalf. Tradition tells us there are seven sins rightly called "deadly," and Dorothy L. Sayers wrote an amusing essay called "The Other Six Deadly Sins." It tells of a young man who asked her in all seriousness what they were. He only knew of one—sexual immorality. This equation of sin and sex is a popular misreading of Paul that was further compounded by the Revised Standard Version of the Bible. Whereas the King James Version translated *porneia* with the earthy word "fornication," the RSV had the euphemism "immorality." Fortunately the NRSV is now more explicit, calling it "sexual immorality."

In her essay, Sayers divides the seven deadly sins into two groups—hot-blooded and cold-blooded sins. In her opinion, and I agree, the cold-blooded sins are much more serious than the hot-blooded ones. Thus anger, lust, and gluttony are easier to understand and forgive than cold-blooded sins like envy, covetousness, sloth or *accidie*—where there is no zest for life—and pride. Once again we meet the idea that hell should be pictured not as a hot place, but as an icebox.

When they do not dispense with them completely, many American Protestants privatize and trivialize sins. Far too often in the popular mind sins are such acts as smoking, drinking, card-playing (especially on Sunday), gambling, or following a different lifestyle. It is an exaggeration, perhaps, but such moralism always reminds me of Jesus' remark to the scribes and Pharisees: "You strain out a gnat but swallow a camel!" The weightier matters of the law, he said, are justice and mercy.

For a view of sin that is far from trivial one should reread the prophets, Jeremiah and Amos in particular. They roundly denounce religious people, especially people who love religious rituals and sacrifices, while they trample on the head of the poor, cheat in business, and "push aside the needy." One of Amos's most eloquent oracles is his familiar complaint against the house of Israel:

> I hate, I despise your festivals
>   and I take no delight in your
>   solemn assemblies.
> Even though you offer me your
>   burnt offerings and grain offerings,
> I will not accept them....

> Take away from me the noise of your songs;
> I will not listen to the melody of your harps.
> But let justice roll down like waters,
>   and righteousness like an
>   ever-flowing stream. (Amos 5:21-24)

This is where the third kind of sin, systemic sin, fits in. The system is out of order and its institutions are corrupt, but we ourselves are part of the system and share responsibility for its ills. We pay taxes and thereby contribute to wars. Many of us live in comfort, ignoring the hungry and the homeless. This is the level on which we need to beg for forgiveness. This is the level on which we "acknowledge one baptism for the forgiveness of sins."

Forgiveness of sins is not the only dimension of baptism, although it is an important one. Baptism is also full initiation by water and the Holy Spirit into Christ's body, the church. It is a sign of new life through Jesus Christ. The fuller meaning of the rite of baptism was set forth in a document issued in 1982 that many believe is the most important ecumenical document to be produced in fifty years, entitled *Baptism, Eucharist, and*

Ministry. Over one hundred theologians representing virtually every major Christian tradition, including Adventist, Pentecostal, and Baptist, along with Roman Catholic, Anglican, Lutheran, Orthodox, and Presbyterian, to name only a part of the list, adopted an agreed-upon statement on the meaning of baptism, eucharist, and ministry. Because the group met in Lima, Peru, the statement is known as the Lima document, or simply *BEM.* The Lima document devotes seven pages to baptism, presenting a comprehensive, many-faceted understanding of what baptism is and does.

The New Testament uses many images to express the reality of baptism and new life. The Lima document highlights five of them: participation in Christ's death and resurrection; conversion, pardon, and cleansing; the gift of the Spirit; incorporation into the body of Christ; and the kingdom of God. Baptism in its full meaning, the statement makes clear, both "signifies and effects" all of these.

The Nicene Creed stresses only the second of these, however, which is the forgiveness of sins. The Lima document recognizes that the baptism administered by Jesus' cousin John was itself a baptism of repentance for the forgiveness of sins (Mk. 1:4). It also cites Hebrews, 1 Peter, Acts, and 1 Corinthians for representing baptism into Christ as having major ethical consequences. It is simultaneously a "washing of the body with pure water" and "a cleansing of the heart of all sin."[2] Furthermore, baptism gives Christians a new ethical orientation, one that calls not only for personal sanctification, but also for striving to realize the will of God in all realms of life.

In the study guide issued by the World Council of Churches to help people explore the new document, the question of why the Nicene Creed specifies *one* baptism is clarified. The document itself merely says that baptism is an unrepeatable act. The study guide asks the question, "Is it defensible in either scripture or tradition to separate two baptisms, one in water and the other in the Spirit?"[3] It points in particular to two accounts in Acts; in one case, some Samaritans had been baptized in the name of the Lord Jesus but had as yet not received the Spirit (Acts 8:6), while in the other, Cornelius and his household received the Spirit first and were baptized afterward (Acts 10). These accounts are in conflict with the Pauline emphasis on one baptism and with the claim that baptism is full initiation with water and the Spirit, as well as in conflict with each other.

At the time of the Reformation the issue of only one baptism surfaced again. Various groups of left-wing reformers rejected the idea that infant baptism was effective and adopted the practice of rebaptizing people who came to be "believers" as adults. These groups were collectively called Anabaptists, a name that means simply "baptizing again." In the course of the conflict over the matter, many Anabaptists were put to death for their custom.

Are you not bristling with questions about these claims? Do you see how any of this applies to a tiny infant who somehow is irrevocably changed just through sprinkling its forehead with a few drops of water and pronouncing the name of the Father, the Son, and the Holy Spirit? Are you happy about the notion that a six-week-old baby is a sinner? *Baptism, Eucharist, and Ministry* has a helpful comment on this last question: "The infant is born into a broken world," it states, "and shares in its brokenness."[4] True, but wouldn't it be better to wait for a person to be able to make an adult decision to be baptized?

A case can be made both for and against infant baptism, and the Lima document summarizes some of the arguments on both sides. Nevertheless, baptism in the early church about the time of Augustine of Hippo must have been a powerful experience, far more powerful than an event you would have been too young to remember. You would have been enrolled as a catechumen for at least a year, and your final preparation for the life-changing event took place in the week before Easter. You fasted and prayed, getting ready for participation in the death and resurrection experience.

Just before midnight on Easter Eve, you would have been taken into the baptistry, stripped naked, immersed completely under water three times, given a new white garment when you came up out of the water, and finally led from the baptistry into the nave of a church ablaze with candles. There, for the first time, you could witness and participate in "the holy mysteries"; as a catechumen, you were not allowed to take part in the Eucharist. You had to leave right after the service of the Word, and the doors were shut behind you.

That, in summary form, is the kind of dramatic baptism I wish we could somehow recover. It would certainly mitigate against "indiscriminate baptism," something *BEM* deplores. Some elements of the ancient liturgy are being reemphasized in modern baptismal rites, especially insistence on the corporate nature of the event. It is not something to be done in the family living room as prelude to a party. The old triple renunciation of the world, the flesh, and the devil is followed by the triple affirmation of faith in God the Father, God the Son, and God the Holy Spirit, using the words of the Apostles' Creed. In newer liturgies the ethical implications of baptism are explicit, such as the promise to strive for justice and peace, and to respect the dignity of every human being.

Holy Baptism is a sacrament, not magic. We will not suddenly become different people after the short service of initiation is over. It is helpful, I think, to borrow a term from John Macquarrie about the nature of a sacrament. He calls it a "focus," an intensification of the divine presence. Do you remember when you first discovered that you could set something afire with a magnifying glass, focusing the sun's rays? Baptism is something like that. God is always ready to forgive, just as the sun's rays always generate heat. As a focus of God's forgiveness, baptism "washes away" our sin, but we need to grow into that clean new life and to ask God's forgiveness for "things done and left undone" over and over again. Jesus taught us to ask God's forgiveness every day in the Lord's Prayer, and he also made it clear that we must forgive others for their offenses against us.

We must not underestimate the cost of forgiveness. Have you ever asked someone's forgiveness and received only a shrug and a "Forget it—it doesn't matter"? You know how unsatisfactory that is. Forgetting and forgiving are not the same thing. God's forgiveness does not mean that God overlooks sin or is indifferent to it. Forgiveness is God's willingness to die for our sins. It is God's running down the road to meet us with open arms to welcome us home. The parable of the Prodigal Son really should be called the parable of the Forgiving Father, and baptism might be described as the first and crucial time of God's running toward us with open arms.

Endnotes

1. Karl Menninger, *Whatever Became of Sin?* (New York: Hawthorn Books, 1973), pp. 14ff.

2. *Baptism, Eucharist, and Ministry*, p. 2. It is noteworthy that one of the latest Faith and Order Papers (No. 153, 1992) is an "Explication of the Apostolic Faith as it is confessed in the Nicene-Constantinopolitan Creed" called *Confessing the One Faith*.

3. William H. Lazareth, *Growing Together in Baptism, Eucharist, and Ministry: A Study Guide*, Faith and Order Paper No. 114 (Geneva: World Council of Churches, 1982), p. 35.

4. *BEM*, p. 5.

Chapter 9

What is Our Future?

*We look for the resurrection of the dead
and the life of the world to come.*

The Nicene Creed makes four affirmations
about the future. In the second paragraph
about Jesus Christ, we asserted that "he will
come again in glory to judge the living and the dead,"
and also that "his kingdom will have no end." Now in
the final paragraph we say, "We look for the resurrection
of the dead, and the life of the world to come." All of
these statements are what theologians call eschatological
ideas, ideas about last or final things. It is here, if any-
where, in the area of eschatological thought, that thinking and questioning Christians should exercise a
reverent agnosticism. We have no blueprint of the future. We have only questions.

Nevertheless, some years ago a Harvard theologian,
Gordon D. Kauffman, still in shock from reading
Jonathan Schell's book on nuclear holocaust, *The Fate of
the Earth*, called on all his academic colleagues to rethink eschatology in the light of a possible all-out nu-

clear war. He called his address "a meditation on nuclear warfare." For Kauffman, none of the traditional symbols fit the new situation we face, the possible end of life on this planet. "We of the late twentieth century are thus sprung loose as a generation," he said, "facing this horrible contingency naked and alone."[1]

The possibility of an all-out nuclear war seems less imminent today than when Kauffman addressed his colleagues, but the danger of our causing irreparable harm to the planet in other ways has grown more acute. The "Earth Summit" in Rio de Janeiro during the summer of 1992 attracted heads of state from all over the world. They sensed the urgency of avoiding environmental disaster. "This fragile earth," as the Book of Common Prayer accurately terms it, is in as great danger from such perils as the destruction of the ozone layer as it is from nuclear holocaust. The idea of a catastrophic end of history was not unknown to biblical faith: God is working God's purpose out and will ultimately triumph over all evil powers, but not before a final battle takes place between good and evil on a cosmic scale, a coming Armageddon. Now humanity faces annihilation by its own hand.

The word "Armageddon" appears just once in the New Testament, in that apocalyptic book called the Revelation to John (16:16), but it has entered into the language as a metaphor for any final struggle or conflict. In the original context, it was the place where the kings of the whole world would assemble for battle on the great day of God the Almighty. Apocalyptic literature itself is something like a Dali surrealist painting, the kind with pocket watches flopped over branches of a dead tree. The apocalyptic books, such as the book of Daniel, are part of a literary genre aptly dubbed "tracts for hard times." The book of Daniel circulated among the Jews during the Maccabbean revolution in 167 B.C.E., a time when the Seleucid emperor Antiochus Epiphanes IV tried to stamp out Judaism. Antiochus desecrated the Temple by sacrificing pigs within the holy precincts, forbade the circumcision of infants, and burned the sacred Torah. Among Jews there was grave anxiety about what the future might hold. In his symbolic visions, Daniel foresees God's direct intervention in history on behalf of his oppressed people. There will come a period of great tribulation, but it will usher in a messianic age, a period of vindication for the Jews.

The book of Revelation, the other major example of apocalypse among the canonical books of the Bible, speaks to a similarly oppressive situation and uses similar apocalyptic imagery. Possibly written during the Roman emperor Domitian's persecution of Christians, it describes the visions that came to John the Seer while he was in exile on the island of Patmos. Addressing his pamphlet to seven churches in the province of Asia, he too foresaw God's direct intervention in history, preceded by a period of great tribulation and culminating in the triumph of good over evil and the arrival of the City of God.

Have you ever tried to read the book of Revelation all the way through? It is admittedly extremely difficult to interpret, yet apocalyptic thought continues to flourish at times when things seem so bad there is widespread despair of them getting any better unless God steps in. Ingmar Bergman's classic film, *The Seventh Seal*, captured the apocalyptic tone during the scenes of the medieval plagues; the widely read novel, *The Four Horsemen of the Apocalypse*, did the same for World War One. Both borrowed their titles directly from the book of Revelation. The questions for apocalyptic thought are, "How can all this suffering and evil come to an end? And will it? When?" Are those not still our questions?

Not all eschatological thought is apocalyptic in nature, however. The idea of the Second Coming of Christ in glory extends far beyond the book of Revelation; almost all the New Testament writers expected an imminent return of Christ to usher in the New Age. They called it the *parousia*, a word that occurs sixteen times in the New Testament. Paul thought the parousia would occur in his own generation, and in 1 Thessalonians he says, "For the Lord himself, with a cry of command, with the archangel's call and with the sound of God's trumpet, will descend from heaven, and the dead in Christ will rise first. Then we who are alive, who are left, will be caught up in the clouds together with them to meet the Lord in the air..." (4:16-17). But he warned the Thessalonians not to try to predict a date. It will come unexpectedly, "like a thief in the night" (5:3).

The unexpected delay of the parousia presented its own problems for early Christian thought. Why was the end delayed? Had the Lord not said that the kingdom of God is "at hand"? Traces of rethinking the imminence of the return of Christ are apparent, for example, in

Luke-Acts, where the Risen Lord tells the apostles that it is not for them to know the time of the Kingdom but clearly links its coming to their first preaching the good news "to the ends of the earth." Within a generation of the first Easter, the expectation that Christ would return any day faded. For the most part, the church settled down for the long haul.

It has never completely lost its sense of eschatological tension, however, at least as long as it observes the liturgical calendar. The season of Advent is a season of intense expectation. Is it merely the anticipation of Christmas? Yes, but also for Christ's coming again. Do you remember that splendid collect which begins, "Stir up thy power, O Lord, and with great might come among us..."? Is that simply waiting for the babe in the manger? Have you ever noticed that the gospel for the first Sunday of Advent is always drawn from that section of the New Testament called "the Synoptic Apocalypse" (Mark 13 and its parallels in Matthew and Luke)? All the Advent gospel readings are based on the theme of the parousia, the second coming of the Son of Man.

Contemporary liturgies have also reintroduced this eschatological tension into our worship. Christian faith is forward-looking; the Eucharist is not merely a commemoration of the Last Supper. Such an acclamation as "Christ has died, Christ has risen, Christ will come again" marks this recognition. It should be noted, however, that Christ's coming need not be imagined with dramatic sound effects; the trumpet of God may not be heard as Christ comes again and again to be present with his people. In an important sense the parousia, the

112

coming of Christ with glory, occurs every time the Eucharist is celebrated. Then the future is present.

The Nicene Creed links the glorious return of Christ closely to his role as judge of the living and the dead, however. Traditionally this has meant the Last Judgment, the final separation of the sheep from the goats, the wheat from the chaff, that will occur in the endtime, the *eschaton*. Matthew's gospel has a vivid account of this judgment: "Come, you that are blessed by my Father, inherit the kingdom prepared for you from the foundation of the world" (25:34). The king's judgment is based on how people have acted toward their unfortunate neighbors: those who did not welcome the stranger, clothe the naked, feed the hungry, or visit the sick and the imprisoned are banished "into the eternal fire prepared for the devil and his angels" (25:41).

The concepts of the devil, and of heaven and hell, are a constant stumbling-block for our secular culture. Is there any reality in any of them? Or are they ancient superstitions that we should discard? The figure of Satan, or the devil, has been around for a long time, at least since the time of Jewish exile in the sixth century, when Persian dualism influenced Hebrew thought. Since then desert hermits have wrestled with him and Milton has immortalized him. Notice that neither the concept of the devil nor the idea of hellfire and damnation is mentioned in the creed. Who or what do you think the devil is today?

Judgment is certainly a part of the creed, however, and so far we have been thinking only in terms of the Last Judgment, the judgment that will occur at the end of time. Christian tradition has also developed the idea of a particular judgment, one that will occur for each of us at the time of clinical death. It is certain, furthermore, that judgment is a continuous process and one we are aware of day by day. Despite all that has been said about the wrath of God, insisting that it is an aspect of God's love, we are not talking about an eye in the sky keeping a score card on each of us. As a wise priest once put it, we judge ourselves in God's presence.

Even as there is a variety of ideas about the timetable of judgment, so too is there some confusion about the kingdom which, according to the creed, "will have no end." The New Testament itself records a variety of opinions. Undoubtedly Jesus' central message was an eschatological one: he announced that the kingdom of God is at hand. This coming reign of God was even then breaking into history. He taught his disciples to pray for its advent, when the will of God will be done on earth. How seriously do you take this petition when you recite the Lord's Prayer? In an article about prayer and our Christian future, Walter Wink takes it with utmost seriousness and writes of intercession as "spiritual defiance of what is, in the name of what God has promised." Intercession, he goes on, "visualizes an alternative future to the one apparently fated by the momentum of current contradictory forces." Indeed, Wink says, "we believe the future into being."[2] Are we really ordering God to bring this reign near when we pray that imperative, "Thy kingdom come, thy will be done, on earth as it is in heaven"?

Often the church has not distinguished between the kingdom of God or the kingdom of Christ. In the Annunciation the angel Gabriel tells Mary that her son will be given the throne of David: "He will reign over the house of Jacob forever, and of his kingdom there shall be no end" (Lk. 1:33). The letter to the Ephesians speaks of the kingdom of Christ and of God, while Colossians calls it the kingdom of God's beloved Son. In 1 Corinthians, however, Paul distinguishes between the two. His discussion of the resurrection puts forward the idea that the kingdom of Christ will last until Christ has put all things under his feet and "then comes the end when he hands over the kingdom to God the Father" (1 Cor. 15:24).

It is worth noting that the Greek text of Paul's letter uses the word *telos* at this point, a word that means goal or purpose. We meet it in the word "teleology," that branch of philosophy that deals with questions of "final causes," of the goal or purpose in natural processes. All eschatological thought is not about a temporal process, a *finis* of everything. It is also about where we are headed.

It is the Apocalypse that sets a timetable for Christ's kingdom. John the Seer claims that Satan will be bound for a thousand years. The martyrs will come to life and reign with Christ for that period. When the thousand years have ended, Satan will be let out of prison for the great last battle (Rev. 20:1-8). Not surprisingly, Christian imagination ran wild over the details of this picture. Two different schools of thought existed about the millennium. One, the so-called pre-millennialist, held that the thousand years followed the Second Coming of Christ. The other school, called post-millennialist, held that the thousand years precedes the Second Coming. The whole subject fell into disfavor with theologians like Augustine of Hippo because of its stress on the bodily pleasures that the saints would enjoy throughout the millennium, and almost disappeared, resurfacing again at the time of the Reformation. Such groups as Seventh Day Adventists and Jehovah's Witnesses still cherish various shades of millennarian thought.

It is easy to see why I think a Christian must stay an agnostic about such matters as the return of Christ and Last Judgment. The same thing needs to be said, and emphatically, about "the resurrection of the dead and the life of the world to come." What will death be like? What will we encounter after death? How can we know?

In late medieval piety the "four last things" were considered to be death, judgment, hell, and heaven. The Dutch painter Hieronymus Bosch painted a vivid picture of each of the four last things around a clock-like depiction of the seven deadly sins. The painting, now in the Prado, shows a deathbed scene. A man lies in bed with clergy in attendance, a monk kneeling at the foot of the bed, a crucifix raised. One of the clergy is reading out of a holy book of prayers, or possibly of Scripture. Atop the bedstead are two little figures—one an angel in white, the other a dark little demon of the kind Bosch is famous for.

The possibility of dying suddenly and unshriven haunted the minds of many Christians at the time.

Thomas Cranmer's Great Litany of 1544 asked that we be delivered from battle, murder, and sudden death. The contemporary version of the same litany changes that last phrase to "dying suddenly and unprepared." Yet in today's world many people dread dying slowly. We make "living wills" to make sure extraordinary measures are not used to prolong our lives. The difference is caused in large part by advances in medical technology, of course, and also by our vastly increased longevity. At the same time, the hospice movement is trying to help people to prepare for death.

No one has done more to rescue the word "death" from euphemisms and from morticians in our time than Elisabeth Kübler-Ross. Death is now something that can and should be talked of openly; the word is no longer taboo. Unfortunately we still encounter obituaries that speak of the deceased as "being taken" or as "passing," not as having died. The biography of Kübler-Ross relates a significant incident in her life, one that helped Christian ministers to deal more honestly with dying patients in the days before most seminarians could take Clinical Pastoral Education. Four seminarians from Chicago Theological Seminary sought out Kübler-Ross in her office and asked for help. They knew that reading from the Bible or reciting set prayers at the bedside of someone at death's door was not enough, but they needed help in going further.

"Death's door" is an antique phrase, obsolescent if not obsolete, but it fits in with Kübler-Ross's idea of a "transition" from life to death. She is better known, however, for the five basic stages we experience in the process of dying, although not necessarily in this order: denial, anger, bargaining, depression, and acceptance. To put it in her words, "I have been able to see the light that my patients see in their near-death experiences, and I have been surrounded by that incredible unconditional love that all of us experience when we make the transition called death."[3]

Have you ever speculated about what state we are in on the other side of that transition? Christians have come up with a variety of ideas. Some talk of the survival of an immortal soul, others of resurrection of the body. Some, in accordance with the idea of judgment, believe that we wait in the grave for the general resurrection at the endtime; others think we pass directly into "the larger life." Some Christians think there is no further chance of growth and change in the new state of being, while others believe we can continue to increase in love and that our choices do not cease.

All of these ideas and others find expression in hymnody and in liturgy, especially in the burial service. The word "immortality" is frequently used to describe this state, but it is a Greek idea, not a Christian one. Immortality implies that there is some part of a human being that is incapable of death, usually the "soul." Resurrection of the body, on the other hand, seems to affirm that we are embodied individuals, psychosomatic selves. You don't *have* a soul; you are a self. The Apostles' Creed specifies a resurrection of the body, but the Nicene Creed does not. The idea of bodily resurrection, however, implies continued personal identity with some recognizable continuity with the previous living human being. The theologian Karl Barth, in one of his intriguing excurses, spoke of his plan to look up Mozart in the new life, to discuss music with him. The notion of reunion with loved ones is pervasive.

The possibility of change and growth in this new state of being are equally controversial. The practice of selling indulgences prior to the Reformation has contributed to Protestant distrust of the notion of an intermediate state for the dead. Indulgences could be gained by the living for souls in purgatory and during the Middle Ages they were grossly abused through unrestricted sale by professional pardoners, with the proceeds going to the church. By buying an indulgence you could, for example, take a year off a family member's time in purgatory.

One of the most effective books on purgatory is C. S. Lewis's *The Great Divorce*. With his gift for graphic description, Lewis tells the tale of a man able to take a bus from hell up to visit his wife in heaven. She keeps offering him a new opportunity to choose love over hate. As he keeps refusing, she sees him visibly shrinking until she finally has to kneel down to look for him among the blades of grass.

The popular images of golden harps, pearly gates, and angelic wings do not help anyone very much in thinking about the resurrection—if indeed they ever did. The idea of eternal rest is not particularly attractive either. Christian tradition does offer us three other ideas about eschatology, however, that throw some light on what is in store for us. Theologians speak of a futurist eschatology, a realized eschatology, and a combination of the two that is sometimes called an "already-but-not-yet" view of the future—more formally, inaugurated eschatology. Although the terms refer properly to the time of the Kingdom, they also have relevance for all questions about "the life of the world to come."

A futurist eschatology clearly implies that everything awaits a consummation that lies ahead of us; it is the object of our hopes, but it is in no way present. Have you ever been haunted by the possibility that the end of the world will occur in your lifetime? I suspect that most of us haven't, but during the height of the Cold War, a friend of mine who is an elementary school teacher told me that most of her fourth-graders did not expect to live to grow up. An indefinite postponement of the coming end is far more appealing. Since we cannot know when it will come, according to the Bible, and since we cannot really imagine what we mean by phrases like "the end of history," this is clearly an attractive choice among eschatological options.

At the other pole is a realized eschatology, one that suggests we already experience all of the resurrection life that is in store for us if we know Jesus Christ and walk in "newness of life" today. This option is also enormously attractive. It resolves any strain toward the future, any sense of anticipation for tomorrow. We have great expectations today. As the old hymn puts it, "New every morning is the love our waking and uprising prove." Why worry about some distant or undesignated future? Why not say simply, "This is the day the Lord has made. We will rejoice and be glad in it"?

The third option is most appealing and, I think, the most biblical. Eternal life begins with baptism, in the death and resurrection that initiation symbolizes. We experience eternal life already in principle, in little flashes, in moments of real worship and times of real love. But we don't already know it in its fullness. The full experience is not yet ours; that gift is given only at clinical death. But we die little deaths and rise to newness of life every day.

One of the most persistent metaphors for life after death is that of a vision, the vision of God. We meet it in Paul's phrase, "Now we see in a mirror, dimly, but then we will see face to face" (1 Cor. 13:12). We meet it in Dante as he is led through paradise with Beatrice as his guide. The beatific vision has always been the goal of the monk and of the mystic, and years ago theologian Kenneth Kirk traced its history in his Bampton Lectures, *The Vision of God*, still a classic in the field. It makes clear that the experience can be a present one, however fleetingly.

As the example of Dante shows, poets are the ones usually able to help us most with thinking about eschatology. A friend of mine, a gifted poet who lives on a farm in Wisconsin, has written a poem on the subject of new vision called "Eschaton":

> I saw the world end yesterday!
> A flight of angels tore
> Its cover off and heaven lay
> Where earth had been before.
> I walked about the countryside,
> And saw a cricket pass.

Then, bending closer, I espied
An ecstasy of grass.[4]

Endnotes

1. Gordon Kauffman, "Nuclear Eschatology and the Study of Religion," *Journal of the American Academy of Religion* 51 (March 1983), p. 11.

2. Walter Wink, "Prayer and the Powers: History Belongs to the Intercessors," *Sojourners* (October 1990).

3. Derek Gill, *Quest: The Life of Elisabeth Kübler-Ross* (San Francisco: Harper & Row, 1980), p. 328.

4. Elizabeth Rooney, "Eschaton," 1978. Quoted by permission of the author.

Chapter 10

What Difference Does
It Make?

T his book has been a series of reflections on the
        questions raised by the Nicene Creed, a
        fourth-century creed still used regularly in
eucharistic worship in churches around the world. It is
about asking questions of the creed for contemporary
Christians and also about learning to delight in the
questions which that summary of the Christian faith
raises in our minds. I have argued that faith accompa-
nied by doubt, articulated doubt, is healthier than faith
that never asks, "Why?"

By virtue of our baptism, all of us are called to be
theologians, called to raise "basic questions about our
inheritance, our identity, and our purpose," as Fredrica
Harris Thompsett has shown so clearly.[1] Asking questions is the method theologians have used for centuries
in order to learn more about God and God's relation to
the world. It was the method that Thomas Aquinas
used in producing his great *Summa Theologica*; each of
the three "parts" of that monumental work includes a
hundred questions to which the Dominican professor

gave his own reasoned answers. Debates about theological questions were also a standard method that theologians like Peter Abelard used in teaching theological students at the University of Paris in the thirteenth century.

Seven centuries later the method of questioning is still widely used in seminary teaching of theology. Owen C. Thomas's sequel to his splendid *Introduction to Theology* is called *Theological Questions: Analysis and Argument*. In the preface Thomas describes his experience of teaching theology by helping students work on questions which have actually arisen in their own lives and work. By giving students practice in asking questions that really interest them, that seem important to them, he reports, "they suddenly realize to their amazement that they can do theology themselves."[2] First-semester seminarians are laypeople, I should remind you, most of whom are total novices in theological inquiry.

In the course of these chapters so far I have raised primarily two kinds of questions, questions of historical theology and questions of contemporary issues and concerns. Both kinds of questions are a help in probing the meaning of the Nicene Creed in the fourth century and today. But there are two additional kinds of questions I want to identify in this final chapter. The first is perhaps the more important, namely, the discovery of your own personal existential questions. The second kind of questions is about the ethical consequences of Christian faith. Theology is always related to ethics, to living the Christian life.

No one can tell you what kinds of questions you have or should have. What seems important for you to think about in connection with the Christian faith and life? One of us may ask more about the natural sciences and religion, for example, whereas another may be more curious about faith and psychology. Or often one has questions of far more personal urgency, born of pain and suffering, of fear or even of joy. A modern Aquinas will ask the questions that occur to him; I have asked questions that occurred to me. One of Owen Thomas's questions is, "What is the relation of sin and neurosis?" while my chapter on sin asked nothing about neuroses because it didn't occur to me. You should feel free to ask anything and everything you want to ask. There is no such thing as a silly theological question, if it is your question.

The Nicene Creed says nothing about the ethical consequences of Nicene faith because ethical issues were not high on the agenda at ecumenical councils in the fourth century. It is different today. That modern creed to which I referred in chapter one included the belief that God the Spirit gives us power "to work for justice, freedom and peace, to smash the idols of church and culture, and to claim all life for Christ."[3] Although such social concerns are not part of the Apostles' Creed, either, they are now explicit in the expanded form of that creed which is part of the baptismal covenant. As the people renew their own baptismal covenant, they are asked, "Will you strive for justice and peace among all people, and respect the dignity of every human being?" Such questions lead urgently to the question,

"How?" How can I work for justice? How can I best contribute to peace? Believing and doing go hand in hand.

After we seek the truth, we are challenged to "do the truth," as John puts it. The three short Johannine epistles are especially fond of the word "truth"; it appears more than fifteen times in the less than five pages these letters take up in the New Testament. Almost invariably it is linked with the word "love." You and I are likely, I think, to associate truth and reason with our heads, but love and emotion with our hearts. We are still victims of a bifurcation in our being that began in the Enlightenment—what T. S. Eliot called the split between sense and sensibility. That split between reason and emotion was manifested in religion as well as elsewhere in our culture.

Our challenge in the late twentieth century is to re-unite our heads with our hearts. The psychiatrist Bruno Bettelheim wrote of the need for this reunion of head and heart among survivors of the Nazi death camps. It was his experience that people in the camps who approached life primarily with the intellect or primarily through the emotions did not survive. Those who relied on both intellect and emotion, who had what he called "an informed heart," made it through the ordeal. What an informed heart means for a Christian is related to our understanding of the three classic theological virtues—faith, hope, and love. Our ethical questions often grow out of these virtues.

We have talked a lot in the preceding pages about faith, usually qualified as the Christian faith. In the creed, however, we do not say "We believe *that*" but "We believe *in*." The difference is tremendous. I can believe that such and such a person is an honest person or a capable physician or a loving kindergarten teacher, but when I trust that person with my money or my health care or my child, I am putting my faith *in* that person. The English language does not make the difference quite as clear as some other languages.

In biblical thought the patriarch Abraham is the prototype of the person of faith. He trusted in God's promises. He set out from Ur in response to God's call, trusting he would find a new homeland. He trusted the seemingly unlikely promise of Sarah's conceiving a child in her old age, a promise that Sarah simply laughed at. The Danish theologian Soren Kierkegaard has written more eloquently about Abraham the Knight of Faith than anyone I know of. In *Fear and Trembling* he invites his reader to take the three days' journey to Mount Moriah with Abraham, on his way to sacrifice his son Isaac. Was Abraham honest with Isaac when he said to him, "God himself will provide the lamb for a burnt offering, my son"?

Trust in God and in God's goodness is different from the so-called "blind faith" people scoff at. It is trust based on the witness of God's revelation of Godself in Jesus Christ, and on the Bible as it witnesses to Christ. But to put one's faith in anyone or anything less than Godself is idolatry, and that includes unadulterated trust in the Bible—the view that finds in the Bible absolute clarity and lack of ambiguity. There is no room for any nuance; it is all written in the holy book. As far as I know the Bible says nothing whatsoever about many contemporary issues, very complex ones such as genetic engineering and organ transplants, but biblical literalists seem to think it contains all the answers. How does such biblicism differ from the dangerous fanaticism easily whipped to a frenzy by any demagogue?

In my opinion, such a vision of what faith entails is clearly incompatible with the other two theological virtues that Paul celebrates—hope and love. A few years ago a forerunner of the liberation theology we talked about earlier attracted considerable attention. It was called "the theology of hope," and one of the most prominent voices in the movement was that of a German theologian, Jürgen Moltmann. As a young man Moltmann was a prisoner of war interned in Britain during World War Two. In a powerful phrase he describes his struggle to retain hope when his horizon was the barbed wire that encircled the camp. "Hope," he says, "rubbed itself raw on the barbed wire."[4] Outside was where freedom lay, out where people lived and laughed. He reports seeing men in the camp who lost hope. Some of them simply lay down, took ill, and died.

Human beings need hope in the future as much as they need faith in someone they can trust. The movement of the theology of hope found philosophical roots in the thought of Ernst Bloch, who spoke of "the ontological priority of the future." More helpfully, he speaks of the pull of the future. That, too, is something we experience all the time, both in short-term and in long-term situations. We write little scenarios about the future in our heads. The horizon of hope lures us forward. That horizon is always moving ahead of us. In a child's drawing, the horizon is usually a straight dark line drawn firmly across the paper; it is static. But go out for a hike or a sail or a drive, and you see it moving ahead of you. What is just around the next bend?

As a Christian virtue, hope involves both the head and the heart. As Moltmann indicated, it is born out of personal experience but it also demands reflection. One of the somewhat surprising injunctions in the New Testament tells the early Christians, "Always be ready to make your defense to anyone who demands from you an accounting for the hope that is in you" (1 Pet. 3:15). One would have expected the author to use "faith" instead. Other translations simply say "to give a reason for the hope that is in you." The word translated "reason" or "defense" is *apologia*. The author of 1 Peter bases Christian hope on Christian experience, too, saying that God has given us a "new birth into a living hope through the resurrection of Jesus Christ from the dead" (1:3).

Perhaps the best-known chapter in the whole New Testament after Luke's infancy narratives is Paul's hymn on love in 1 Corinthians 13. A few years ago I went to an off-Broadway play, a rock opera version of the book of Jonah that was written by a young Jew. The music was loud but nevertheless the singing was a moving retelling of the tale almost verbatim. But somewhat incongruously, the young singer in an epilogue sang softly, also verbatim, Paul's hymn to love: "If I speak in the tongues of mortals and of angels..." and ending,

"And now faith, hope, and love abide, these three, and the greatest of these is love."

The English word "love" covers a multitude of attitudes and relationships. It is an omnibus word used for everything from the vows one makes at the altar to feelings about chocolate cake. As is often the case, other languages have more than one word to distinguish more sharply what is meant. C. S. Lewis wrote on *The Four Loves* to distinguish among affection, friendship, sexual love, and God's love, using the four different Greek words for these relationships. Affection is a love based on familiarity. You may feel affection for someone whose habits often annoy you, in fact. Friendship is a far deeper and stronger bond, and far more selective. You choose your friends. For Lewis it was the group of Oxford writers, "The Inklings," who drank beer together in the pub on Tuesdays and gathered in Lewis's rooms on Thursdays to read their own new writings to each other.

The third and fourth types of love are *eros* and *agape* in the Greek. Often theologians have distinguished sharply between them, and that was the case in a highly acclaimed work, *Agape and Eros*, by Anders Nygren, a Swedish bishop. In his discussion of the two terms, Nygren faulted Augustine for mixing the two up and combining them in a single Latin word, *caritas*, from which we get "charity." Nygren makes the same criticism in his commentary on Romans. When Paul writes, "God's love has been poured into our hearts through the Holy Spirit that has been given us" (5:5), Nygren argued, Paul is speaking of God's love for us, not of our love for

God. But Augustine thought otherwise. Indeed, he found in the text from Romans support for his teaching that grace infuses love into human beings, so that they are empowered to love God and their neighbor. Nygren charges that Augustine has more of *eros* than of *agape* in it. Just another quibble over words? Not really. The total separation of human love from divine love is unwarranted.

Although *eros* meant primarily sexual love, Plato had already spiritualized it, using the term of the upward striving of the human being for the divine. Human beings may by nature be inclined to "hate" God, as the old Heidelberg Catechism claimed, but when Jesus gave us the command to "love the Lord your God with all your heart, and with all your soul, and with all your mind, and with all your strength" (Mk. 12:29), he certainly is speaking of human response to the prior love of God. Nygren was indeed "rather cavalier," as one critic put it, in pressing the total distinction between *agape* and *eros*.

Erotic love in the sense of sexual love is, in fact, sacramental in nature. The sad distortion of the Christian faith Dorothy L. Sayers noted in her essay, "The Other Six Deadly Sins," is again the target in her essay, "The Dogma is the Drama," written in catechism form:

> Q. What does the Church think of sex?
> A. God made it necessary to the machinery of the world, and tolerates it, provided the parties are (a) married and (b) get no pleasure out of it.[5]

Compare that with the tradition which holds that marriage is a sacrament and that the propagation of the species is not the sole purpose of marriage. God uses the physical to communicate the spiritual. People who think otherwise about sex must be unaware of the erotic love poetry in Holy Scripture, the Song of Songs, which was *not* written as an allegory about Christ and his church.

Have you ever thought of God as Lover? Sallie McFague tries out that metaphor in her thought-provoking book, *Models of God*. She is properly critical of the Greek tradition in Christian thought about God—that God is "without body, parts, and passions," as the Thirty-Nine Articles of Religion expresses it. The Greek idea of a God who could not suffer dominated Christian thought for centuries. God could indeed love; in fact, God *is* love. But to picture God as Lover was virtually unknown outside the mystic tradition.

Seeking to reintroduce speaking of God as Lover, as *eros*, McFague points out that the love relationship is the deepest of human relationships and that "the crux of love is not lust, or desire."[6] Rather, she says, the crux is *value*. Lovers love each other because they find each other valuable, not because of their beauty or their intelligence, and not because they have hopes of changing the other. If God is lover, on this reasoning, God loves us and values us, all of us, just as we are. God finds us valuable, worthy of love.

Worship, it should be remembered, means "giving worth to." Usually, of course, the word refers to worshiping a deity, but it used to have a wider reference. In the older marriage services, at the exchange of rings, the man said to the woman, "With this ring, I thee wed; with my body, I thee worship."

Christian faith, hope, and love issue in Christian worship. Worship expresses our faith in God, our hope in God's future, our love of God's very Self, Father, Son and Holy Spirit. But worship not only expresses these dimensions of the Christian life, it also evokes them. It helps create faith and hope and love that are integral parts of being a Christian in the world. Worship helps to expand "our hearts into a world-embracing space of healing from which no one is excluded."[7]

This quotation is from a remarkable little book on compassion, in which the three co-authors see the close link between prayer and action. They rightly insist that the Eucharist is at the heart of Christian worship, that each time we come together around the bread and the wine we gain an inkling of God's purpose for humanity. We are called to learn to care about the welfare of the whole world, to be fully aware of the pain and suffering around the world—and to do something about it. Action goes hand in hand with worship.

Eucharistic worship is the context in which together we recite the Nicene Creed. Because of this context, the creed transcends the ancient controversies that first brought it into being. In that context it is also more than a summary of the Christian story; it becomes a doxology, an act of praise of God's glory, of God's very nature. And then we are sent out to love and serve the Lord.

What difference does the creed make? It helps lead us to respond to God's world by loving the world God has made, and all the people in it.

Endnotes

1. Fredrica Harris Thompsett, *We are Theologians* (Cambridge, MA: Cowley Publications, 1989), p. 1.

2. Owen C. Thomas, *Theological Questions: Analysis and Argument* (Wilton, CT: Morehouse-Barlow, 1983), p. 9.

3. "A Proposed Statement," p. 152.

4. Jürgen Moltmann, foreword to M. Douglas Meeks, *Origins of the Theology of Hope* (Philadelphia: Fortress Press, 1974), p. x.

5. Dorothy L. Sayers, *Creed or Chaos* (New York: Harcourt, Brace, 1949), p. 22.

6. McFague, *Models*, p. 127.

7. Donald P. McNeill, Douglas A. Morrison, and Henri J. M. Nouwen, *Compassion* (Garden City, NY: Doubleday, 1983), p. 109.

C owley Publications is a ministry of the Society of St. John the Evangelist, a religious community for men in the Episcopal Church. Emerging from the Society's tradition of prayer, theological reflection, and diversity of mission, the press is centered in the rich heritage of the Anglican Communion.

Cowley Publications seeks to provide books, audio cassettes, and other resources for the ongoing theological exploration and spiritual development of the Episcopal Church and others in the body of Christ. To this end, it is dedicated to developing a new generation of theological writers, encouraging them to produce timely, creative, and stimulating publications of excellence, and making these publications available widely, reaching both clergy and lay persons.